A MAN WHO SAVED AMERICA

Premium Edition

Basil E. Pinker

This book is dedicated to The Great Creator, those who initiate, those who implement, and those who follow.

CONTENTS

Title Page

Copyright

Dedication

Chapter 1   1

Chapter 2   4

Chapter 3   10

Chapter 4   13

Chapter 5   16

Chapter 6   19

Chapter 7   21

Chapter 8   24

Chapter 9   28

Chapter 10   34

Chapter 11   39

Chapter 12   44

Chapter 13   49

Chapter 14   54

Chapter 15   56

Chapter 16   59

Chapter 17   63

Chapter 18   65

Chapter 19   68

Chapter 20   71

Chapter 21   74

Books By This Author   75

CHAPTER 1

It is said of mankind that five percent are initiators, ten percent are ones who implement, and the remaining eighty-five percent are followers. Or, said another way, the artificial world we live in originates from the creativity of just five percent of the population, and these individuals, more often than not, exist and operate away from the public eye. The public figures we so often associate with leadership, more often than not, are *not* initiators, but ones who implement. Ones who implement take ideas originating from initiators and, supervising teams of followers, turn them into reality. Followers are content to live and work as they are told, probably because it is the easiest path and one that causes the least friction.

Perhaps this explains why the man who saved America was not President Robert Cotton, although he was more than happy to take the credit, but rather an eccentric West Virginia trillionaire by the name of Dr. Ben Nelson.

In the year that President Cotton was inaugurated, The United States of America was over 50 trillion dollars in deficit, and approximately four times that figure in debt. The only reason that the USA continued to exist and out of default was that the rest of the world was in worse financial shape. The rest of the world depended on the USA to help service their debts, and the USA was more than happy to print money to accomplish this. The situation had progressed far past the breaking point, and the entire civilized world was being held together by a mere thread.

President Cotton was elected to remedy this problem. He ran his campaign on this issue. He gave an uplifting inaugural speech with glowing words and esteemed promises. He sounded confident and convincing. "Fear no longer lives in our house!" President Cotton said. But he had no real answers.

Human nature had taken hold of the USA and rest of the world at large. Greed and corruption had overpowered frugality, common sense, and goodness. Control was in the hands of power hungry buffoons. Living beyond one's means was not only practiced at large, it was expected...even taught in schools. Runaway inflation crippled everyone's life style, but most of all the ones who could least afford the extra cost. The meek were far from inheriting the earth, and there was no foreseeable way out.

"How do we give the best impression to our fellow American Citizens that we are on top of this crisis?" President Cotton asked his newly appointed Joint Council for Economic Affairs. "This problem is everybody's problem, and we need answers."

The Chairman of the Federal Reserve, Olivia Wilkens, was the first to respond. "I see no easy answers avoiding extreme hardship. The obvious solutions would most certainly project an image of anti-growth, eliminations and weakness. God forbid that the most powerful nation on Earth be seen as a shrinking super power! My best advice is to outpace the debt interest burden through money creation."

"But isn't that how we got here in the first place?" President Cotton asked.

"True, but at present, I'm afraid it is all we've got." Chairperson Wilkens responded. "The borrowing has grown so large, I don't see how to pay it back without some revolutionary change, which would not be well received politically. We can, however, proceed and succeed by staying one step ahead. Project a positive good-faith message, demonstrate progress and pray for a miracle. Have faith in America, Mr. President. We've been through tougher times."

Next to respond was Robert Phillips, Director of the Internal

Revenue Service. "Money creates money. A trillion dollars appreciates by 10 billion a year on average. We simply need $500 trillion to service our present deficit."

Everyone laughed uncomfortably.

"Unfortunately it is no longer a joke." Director Phillips continued. "The Federal Government does not own appreciating assets per se. There is that stock pile of gold bullion sitting in Fort Knox. Money, however, no longer is tied to the value of gold directly. I'm not sure what purpose there is to owning gold, particularly when its value would only scratch the surface toward solving the monetary crisis we now face. Perhaps our best bet is to somehow find a way to tap the ingenuity and productivity of the private sector."

"Maybe it is time for a digital currency." Chairperson Wilkens suggested. "That would give us control over interest rates beyond our present capabilities."

"That may be the way of the future," President Cotton responded, "But security is a challenge. Hackers almost robbed us of our most recent election. It is not a stretch to imagine cyber-thieves destroying the entire system. The damage they could do potentially would be far worse than robbing a bricks-and-mortar bank. And what about emergency power grid outages?"

"We already are attempting to address overspending." President Cotton continued. "Imagine how the public will react to additional unprovoked financial burdens such as negative interest rates when they already are shouldering a heavy tax burden plus inflation. It would be too tempting and a slippery slope to negotiate."

CHAPTER 2

On a misty morning in May, two black SUVs with federal government license plates arrived in downtown Elkins, West Virginia stopping at the main filling station. Two of the five gentlemen riding in these vehicles stepped inside the attached convenience store, while the others made use of the restroom facilities after a long ride.

"Pardon me," The lead gentleman spoke to the attendant standing behind the counter. "Can you tell me where I might find Dr. Ben Nelson?"

"Are you serious?" The attendant answered. "What business would you happen to have with our local town kook?

"Don't get smart with me kid. Our business is confidential." The gentleman snapped, flashing his government identification badge. "Internal Revenue Service. Agent Parkins."

"Well, if you insist on wasting your time, you'll likely find Dr. Nelson up the road and two blocks over." The attendant said. "He's a bit of a weirdo, as you will find. Claims he's a trillionaire. Really doesn't act like one. Look at where and how he lives and what he drives. Your average everyday millionaire would appear to fare much better, and we don't have many if any of them around in these parts. Well, you'll see."

"Thanks for your help." The IRS Agent replied and swiftly departed.

Minutes later, arriving at the intended destination, the government men found a sixty-something-year-old man with a graying beard seated in an Adirondack chair outside toying with a cell phone.

"Wondered when you fellows would show up." The gentleman spoke. "Ben Nelson here. Anything I can do for you?"

"We are Internal Revenue Service Agents, and we would like a word with you. We are hoping for your cooperation." The lead agent said. "My name is Agent Smith and this here is Agent Tucker."

"Nice to meet you, " Nelson replied. "Don't know if I am happy about it though."

"We get that a lot." Smith said.

"What took you so long?" Nelson asked. "Received word that you were on your way up here about a half hour ago. When something out of the ordinary happens in these parts, news travels quickly."

"Took a pit stop downtown." Smith answered. "We certainly could use some of that communication efficiency in the Agency."

"The reason we are here is twofold." Smith continued. "Naturally we are here to collect on overdue income taxes owed plus penalties. Perhaps more importantly, we are here to learn just how you acquired such a high level of taxable income in such a short period."

"I am grateful for your interest in my affairs." Nelson said and chuckled softly. "However I'm not certain that giving you my money is a wise choice. Your track record for handling public funds is pretty awful."

"We just collect the money," Agent Smith said. "That is our job. Elected officials are responsible for misuse of what is collected. Anyway, your tax bill is remarkably large and payment is needed soon."

"What bothers me is that that does nothing toward correcting the fundamental problem." Nelson said. "The government has spent so far beyond its means that future generations have been robbed. Where is the justification for that? And what do we have to show for it?"

"It is hard to argue with you on that, but I still have a job to do." Smith answered. "Can you explain how your taxable income went from zero last tax year to over a trillion dollars for the present reporting tax year? We have records from your broker showing over 1.2 trillion dollars in profitable income."

"Well I can explain that," Nelson answered, "but it will take some time. Can we arrange a meeting to consider the matter in the near future? I am willing to settle my tax bill, but there are conditions that I would like to be considered and hopefully met."

"Fair enough." Smith countered. "I only have limited flexibility here, but I will inform my boss of your wishes."

"Good!" Nelson chirped. "I have given the matter a great deal of thought already, and have drafted a list of conditions. My upmost priority is confidentiality. We are not at a point where this can be disclosed to the public."

"Our policy is strict abidance by level-three classification and need-to know protocols." Agent Smith stated. "Is there any specific problem?"

"Well, let me ask you then," Dr. Nelson inquired. "What would you do if you discovered a rare gem valued at say a trillion dollars?"

There was a prolonged pause. No immediate answer was offered.

"Have you ever wondered what you would do in such a situation?" Nelson continued. "Where would you go to convert the gem to transaction-able currency? How many trillionaires or trillion-dollar businesses are there out there to complete the transaction?"

More silence.

"Or, what if I gave you a trillion dollar bill? Where would you take it to receive change?"

"Is it possible to have too much wealth?"

More silence.

"Now consider becoming known as the person possessing this wealth." Dr. Nelson continued. "How does such a person manage to live a respectable private life with this much wealth. Is there not a responsibility to put the wealth to good use at solving worldly problems? And which are most important? How can one elevate the standard of living of humankind most effectively?"

"Our problems are magnitudes below that level." Agent Smith responded. "I've never dreamed of confronting such issues."

"Nor I before my recent discovery " Dr. Nelson said. "I once was asked what I did for a living at a local pub."

"Nothing at the moment." I responded without thinking having had a few beers. "I'm worth a trillion dollars."

"As you might imagine, that is how I earned the title of *town kook*." Dr. Nelson continued. "I was partly curious how such news would be received. And knowing what I know now, I would have answered differently...lied even. It was quite a scene that night, and, of course word travels quickly in this town. No one took me serious fortunately. But I've never let anyone else know of my financial status. Don't really know quite how."

"It is why I've been reluctant to report my income status to the IRS. I knew eventually you would come to me, and that would permit at least a modicum of confidentiality."

"Consider discovering a repeatable method for generating trillion dollar profits." Dr. Nelson continued. "Should I share this with the world or keep it to myself and/or a select few? What if this knowledge ended up in the wrong peoples' hands? Can you imagine the damage that might cause? And would I be partly responsible for making that possible?"

"What if every person I ever knew showed up on my door step asking for a hand out?"

Silence.

"I could auction the method to the highest bidder. That ultimately would be selfish and limiting, but personally rewarding."

"I could sell it as a money-making plan. But consider the competition and the absurdity. Imagine a trillionaire offering to sell his great secret for how to make money. Obviously, the trillionaire doesn't need to sell anything to earn money. If he did, it would mean his money making plan probably doesn't work. Who would believe him?"

"Your questions are above my pay grade." Agent Smith replied.

"I could write a book or teach classes." Nelson continued. "That leads to other potential problems. My plan might only succeed because it has not yet been discovered by others and widely practiced. Great discoveries often are accidental and most rewarding to the first few individuals who participate. If I taught a class of pupils how to make a trillion dollars, would their implementation of the method dilute the strength of its initial success?"

"You have given this a great deal of thought." Agent Smith said. "I'm beginning to understand your position and am a little grateful to not be in your shoes."

"Indeed I have." Nelson countered. "It keeps me awake at night wondering what's best to do."

"My discovery has the potential to do a great deal of good for mankind, which is my highest intention." Dr. Nelson continued. "But wouldn't it be awful to kill the golden goose in the process? What if once word got out and people started using this method to their benefit, the regulatory authorities stepped in to make it more difficult to implement, or ultimately abolished the mechanisms that made it work?”

“That seems to happen a lot.” Agent Tucker interjected.

“Power corrupts.” Nelson continued. “I'd hate to lose the value of the discovery to people of limited vision. Only those who live in a world of limitations are needful of lording over others. Those who recognize that we live in a world of limitless possibilities, they are the ones most free. But, I digress”

“I have drafted a proposal for you to take back with you to Washington.” Dr. Nelson said. “I am attaching a blank signed check drawing on the account where my profits reside. You can fill in the numbers for the amount you require.”

“This is highly irregular procedure.” Agent Smith said. “We require your Income Tax Return.”

“Take it or leave it.” Dr. Nelson responded without concern. “It appears that you are the ones with the fiscal problem. You need my help. And I just might have the answer you are looking for.”

“Again I will run it by my boss.” Agent Smith said. “But you have to know you are asking a lot. Very few get such special treatment.”

“And you have to know that I am offering a lot.” Dr. Nelson replied. “No one I know has achieved a trillion dollar income.... let alone in one year. You can cash my check and drain my account to zero. I can and will have the money back within another year. Knowledge is power you can't take away.”

The agents looked at each other and shrugged.

“Accept my offer and everybody wins.”

CHAPTER 3

The proposal that Dr. Nelson drafted was a real eye opener. It required a special convention of the three branches of the United States government to address with President Cotton presiding. The gathering to consider and approve this proposal was similar to the annual State-of-the-Union Presidential-address gathering. As such, there were some procedural issues to entertain and modify to make the conduct of business possible.

"My fellow Senators, House Representatives, and Justices of the Supreme Court of the United States of America," President Cotton began, "We are gathered here today to conduct the business of the American Public. Our situation is dire. Our present course of action is unsustainable. And time has now come to correct our heading for the purpose of building a robust and prosperous future."

"I will not dwell on how we got here, or how we have robbed future generations of freedom and standard of living. I stand here today to posit a solution."

"It goes against human nature to cut back, to reduce, to eliminate. The sheer size of Government expansion reflects the yearning of the human soul to develop, and grow and prosper. No one appears to be serious about living within a defined budget, no matter how generous. And frankly, if an ordinary citizen practiced the welcoming of indebtedness that the institutions of our government enjoy and practice, he or she would soon find themselves in prison for malfeasance."

"We are here to serve the American Public....not to misrepresent or mis-serve them. It is time to become responsible adults and face our challenge purposely and directly. To that end, I have called this special session, and am issuing an Executive Order directing this body to legislate a successful path enabling the swift completion of meeting the specified goals. Each of you has been provided with a copy of the conditions to be addressed."

"Ladies and gentlemen, we have been approached with a proposal which has the promise to address and solve the primary problem, or problems that have brought us to where we are today. We have a citizen, who prefers to remain anonymous, who has accomplished something remarkable. He has become a trillionaire within a year, demonstrating that America truly is the Land of Opportunity. This thoughtful and caring citizen has offered to spearhead a special mission to pay off the debts of the United States before our present congressional term is ended."

The entire chamber buzzed with murmuring, giggling and excitement.

"Imagine returning our great country to prosperity! Imagine carrying forward on solid financial footing the greatness we yet can accomplish. This is now within our grasp."

"Our future prosperity comes with conditions. I have called us together to set about working toward the meeting of these conditions. Some may not like what is asked of us. The reward however is too great to pass up, and it is we who presently are at the disadvantage."

"Recall the Manhattan Project enabling the ending of World War II. Recall the Apollo Moon Landing which won the Space Race and contributed to the ending of the Cold War. Today we face a similar challenging opportunity. Our undefeatable spirit demands that we now accept that challenge."

"Within the Executive Branch I have established a new Bureau of Deficit Reduction and am presently gathering a list of qualified candidates to consider for the appointment of Director. Your cooperation in providing a speedy approval is requested and expected."

"The constitutional changes necessary to meet the conditions before you are the duty of the Legislative Branch. Let this important task proceed speedily, as well, and followed by a thorough review and approval by the Supreme Court and Judicial Branch. I stand ready to sign the resulting legislature into law."

"My fellow colleagues, we have work to do. Let us proceed accordingly. America is counting on us. God Bless The United States of America."

CHAPTER 4

The conditions to be addressed, drafted by Dr. Ben Nelson, were not insignificant. Dr. Nelson insisted on getting the conditions addressed before getting to work on drawing down the National Debt. In lieu of remitting his personal income tax owed, Dr. Nelson became Chief Consulting Officer for the Patriot Project within the Bureau of Deficit Reduction. His service would last until the Bureau Mission was accomplished, or until the National Deficit was eliminated. His identity remained unknown to everybody except a select few IRS agents and need-to-know Bureau employees. At the start, even President Cotton was kept out of the loop, a condition requested and required by Dr. Nelson.

Dr. Nelson proposed the initiation of the Patriot Project upon the enactment of a minimum of five of the seven conditions presented. The conditions to be addressed were as follows beginning with a short preamble.

Preamble to the Patriot Project

The founding fathers of The United States of America never intended the practice of representative government to be a full time job. They never intended elected officials to occupy permanent career positions. They never intended for elected officials to enrich themselves beyond the position salary level while serving in elected office.

The founding fathers never intended for elected representatives to live beyond their budgetary means or practice poor stewardship of public funds. They never intended public officials to enact legislation impacting issues extending beyond their active term of service in office without periodic review for continuing necessity. They never intended the establishment of tyranny after fighting a Revolutionary War to establish independence from tyranny.

The following conditions are offered to re-establish government to an entity more in line with the vision of the founding fathers.

Condition 1. Balanced Budget

Government spending shall not exceed appropriated annual levels except in cases of national emergency. Emergency spending shall be repaid to the public treasury via appropriation reductions when possible.

Condition 2. Term Limits

No citizen can serve more than two elected terms for the offices of President, Vice President, Senator, House Representative, Senate Majority Leader, Senate Minority Leader, Speaker of the House, or House Minority Leader. No citizen may serve consecutive terms in the same elected position.
Appointed Supreme Court Justices may serve a single 12-year term. Elected Presidents shall have the honor of appointing at least three Supreme Court Justices to replace those with expiring terms.
No elected or appointed official shall be allowed to campaign for elected office while presently serving an active term.

Condition 3. Elections

The elective process shall last no longer than six months. Citizens may not run for any elected office after reaching the age of 70 years without passing a cognitive fitness test.

Condition 4. Service

Elected and appointed officials may not accept payments from outside sources while serving in office. Elected officials, appointed officials and immediate family members may not purchase or sell private sector stock shares or private investments during their active term.

Condition 5. Legislative

There shall be no enactment of laws extending beyond the active congressional term. No bills shall be passed or signed unread and not duly deliberated

Condition 6. Taxes

Taxing income shall be made illegal. The income tax code shall be abolished and replaced with a flat consumption tax.

Condition 7. Compensation

Salaries of elected and appointed federal officials shall be pegged to the National Prosperity Index. Raises in salary shall only be furnished in years of economic growth.

CHAPTER 5

It is said of mankind that when two or more individuals or social groups meet, one of three outcomes result. (1) They fight, or compete. (2) They exchange goods, services, and/or ideas, or cooperate. (3) They reproduce.

The developing relationship of Dr. Nelson with the U.S. Government demonstrated behavior exemplifying the second outcome above.

Dr. Nelson remained in West Virginia going about his private life while the Government deliberated, argued, whined, fretted, yelled, cried, and postured over his proposed conditions, or demonstrated behavior exemplifying the first outcome above.

Dr. Nelson was odd in more than one way. He earned a Ph.D. in Plant Science more or less just to see what that experience was like. He wasn't particularly enamored with the discipline he chose. He never published a professional paper after completing his dissertation and never worked in a Plant Science teaching or research position. Although competent enough, his interests drifted elsewhere.

Dr. Nelson loved puzzle solving. To him life was a great big puzzle. To him the working world was a contrivance of economic enslavement. No job working for another ever offered compensation enough in exchange for the hours of life energy required and expended. If it did, then someone else was positioned disadvantageously to make such compensation possible.

To Dr. Nelson the financial world was the biggest and most intriguing puzzle of all. This basically is how he succeeded at earning over one trillion dollars in a single year. Put simply, Dr. Nelson found a workable solution to the big financial puzzle.

Not only did Dr. Nelson discover how to make money in the financial markets, it appeared that he discovered how to do it without putting other participants at a necessary disadvantage. Dr. Nelson remained uncertain that such a result was possible, but thought it wise to keep his discovery confidential to avert possible disaster. Putting others at a disadvantage for personal gain was something Dr. Nelson deeply shunned. It was why he knew he never would make a good salesman. He was too empathetic.

Interestingly, Dr. Nelson managed to acquire a trillion dollars with no adverse market reaction. He did so with no negative consequences that he could discern other than a visit from the IRS.

"Perhaps this discovery is something special after all." He thought.

The wheels of government turn slowly. It was six months before the conditions Dr. Nelson proposed became the law of the land, five of them anyway. Congress was still hammering away at the remaining two conditions, but they looked likely to pass also. The benefits from the enactment of the five conditions required began to show results almost immediately. There was growing optimism among the American Public once word got out that improvement was possible. Pressure was kept on the elected representatives to complete what they had started.

Conditions 5 and 6 were still under deliberation when Dr. Nelson was notified of the progress. Condition 5 focused on the Legislative Branch and stated that 'There shall be no enactment of laws extending beyond the active congressional term. No bills shall be passed or signed unread and not duly deliberated.' Condition 6 focused on Taxes and stated 'Taxing income shall be made illegal. The income tax code shall be abolished and replaced with a flat consumption tax.'

The Government was having trouble giving up power and Conditions 5 and 6 demanded this. Passing laws for establishing programs that never went away even after they had outgrown their usefulness was a way of life for the Government. Accountability was not. Simplifying the tax code was beyond anyone's functionality. Downsizing and re-purposing IRS business, while good for the country, meant diminishing Government authority, which never sat well with those in power.

President Cotton's executive order placed a freeze on Government spending with the aim at reducing overall government size by 10 percent. The means by which the reduction would take place was to be natural staffing attrition accompanied by no new hiring, no program expansions, and no project additions. The freeze was to remain in place until the the Federal Budget was back in balance.

The achievement of meeting the five required conditions set forth by Dr. Nelson meant that the time had come to bring Dr. Nelson to Washington, D.C. and get started on Patriot Project business. As straight forward as that sounded, there remained a few wrinkles to iron out. In comparison to what changes had already taken place, these few wrinkles were relatively minor and would be addressed in due course.

CHAPTER 6

Back in the White House during the next meeting of the Joint Council for Economic Affairs, Chairperson Wilkens brought up the first matter of pressing concern.

"Mr. President," Wilkens began. "We need a review and consent order for the legality of the US Government to purchase and sell equity index options. It is not legal for the Government to purchase and sell private sector corporate stock because of conflict of interest. But is it legal for the Government to buy and sell market index options on open market exchanges? The Bureau of Deficit Reduction is in need of a prompt answer."

"Draft and present the order for my signature as soon as possible." President Cotton directed. "Is this related to the Patriot Project?"

"Indeed." Wilkens answered. "Everything...the success and failure of our republic...our very survival may depend on the Government's ability to participate in equity index option trading."

"It's an interesting consideration." IRS Director Phillips added. "The open markets collectively are made up of private enterprise entities. Taken together, the buying and selling of equity index options represents not so much a bet on the success of any one single enterprise, an obvious conflict of interest issue, but rather a bet on the success and/or failure of a significant portion of the entire economy. This includes many international enterprises."

"Understandably, betting against one's own well being would represent a conflict. But is betting in favor of collective success to be discouraged? Are market neutral strategies that promote more efficient functioning markets problematic? I believe the case can be made for Government participation in market equity index option trading."

"I am certainly no economic expert." President Cotton said. "But if I understand you correctly, Government participation in market activity that it also regulates can be beneficial under specific conditions?"

"Correct, Mr. President." Philips responded. "The Government could assume a role similar to the market makers, those who buy and sell securities to ensure a smooth market operation. Buying and selling market equity index options entails no direct private enterprise ownership. There is no 'security' representative of the market value per se. The option to participate in the increase and/or decrease in overall market valuation can and is traded daily on the open market. Such options are cash paid derivatives of market index settlement value relative to expiration that have no other valuation or privilege."

"I'm not sure exactly what that means," President Cotton said. "But it sounds like a win-win. It certainly sounds complex enough to be debated for years. All we need is to initiate the Patriot Project while applying for legal approval. Should we succeed by the time that approval is obtained, then it will have been proven useful already. And if approval is rejected, it will be difficult to argue against prosperity."

CHAPTER 7

"The Patriot Project invites you to become a part of History." Project Director Mark Bailey began addressing a small group of civil servant employees. "You have been carefully selected and pre-accepted to participate in the restoration of American prosperity. With your approval you will be provided with confidential instructions defining your specific duties and objectives. Your cooperation is voluntary, but strictly conditional. Beginning now, you have 24 hours to make your decision."

"Those of you deciding to proceed will be required to sign and file a nondisclosure agreement. Until further notice, nothing revealed to you associated with this project shall be disclosed to outside entities, and that includes all entities that are not associated with the Patriot Project."

"You are being asked to put the interests of your country ahead of your own personal interests for an indeterminate period. Your skills and talents are needed and a special bonus is to be included in your compensation. The success of the Patriot Project imperatively requires utmost secrecy in execution until our primary objective is reached. Hopefully, America can count on you."

The candidate selection process performed beyond expectations. The mystery of what was to be revealed combined with the opportunity to be a part of something positive and larger than oneself was too much to resist. Unanimous acceptance by chosen candidates resulted and The Patriot Project proceeded to its next stage of implementation.

"Welcome to The Patriot Project!" Director Bailey began, addressing the newly accepted project participants. "Today we begin our work toward solving the American deficit problem. Like our business activities, our location will remain undisclosed to outside entities until further notice."

"We will begin with a brief introduction of the *Money Catcher Strategy* upon which our future success depends. The *Money Catcher Strategy* was discovered by Dr. Ben Nelson, who has agreed to join us today, and who will say a few words momentarily. Dr. Nelson has successfully grown an options trading account to over one trillion dollars and has done so in less than one tax year. He has authored a white paper fully describing the methodology... a copy of which sits in front of you for your perusal. You may not take a hard copy of this white paper outside our secured area."

"There are three areas of concern until we get a better understanding of how this method works. First, we have no history at this time to tell us how the open market will react when we scale up implementation. Greater market-participation activity might lead to dilution of efficacy. It might as likely lead to improved market order flow. Or it might have no discernible effect."

"Second, the market regulators, beyond our control, might decrease strategy success by altering acceptable spread widths or other necessary parameters. This will be discussed further in future meetings, but essentially success might lead to forced failure."

"Third, the less outside interference, or competition, the better, at least initially. So we shall proceed with utmost confidentiality and caution."

"We at first considered forming a group of trading patriots. Following a specific set of instructions, a trusted group of colleagues thereby would implement the strategy in duplicity. Upon further study, it became clear that repeatable duplicity is what computers were designed for. This is why we have recruited computer programming specialists. The ideal objective is to automate the process so as to require minimal monitoring or hands-on activity. So that is where we are headed."

"With that said, Dr. Nelson the floor is yours."

"Greetings fellow patriots." Dr. Nelson began. "I am Dr. Ben Nelson, and it appears that I am the reason that we are here today. Public speaking makes me nervous...so bear with me."

"It appears that I have achieved something that no other known trader, retail or institutional, has achieved. I took a rather ordinary personal brokerage trading account from a starting value of $5,000 to a finishing value of over one trillion dollars. To my knowledge, no one has ever done this before."

"As remarkable as this sounds, it gets better. Once the method was refined, I was able to reach the trillion dollar level in less than one year. And everything was done using a rather ordinary cell phone."

"In essence, I traded, or rather day-traded, a form of *Option Butterfly Combination* associated with underlying assets that met specific market requirements. You will learn the specifics as we progress toward project implementation."

"The Patriot Project will progress in three straight-forward phases; the instructional, the developmental, and the implementation. Before we can carry out a coordinated plan of execution, we must educate ourselves in the fundamentals and understand how to put the pieces together. I look forward to seeing you in our next session where we will begin the instructional phase."

CHAPTER 8

"The *Money Catcher Strategy* employs buying and selling *Skinny Butterfly Option Combinations* associated with underlying assets meeting specific criteria." Dr. Nelson began leading the discussion as the instructional phase got started. "By now you have had time to study the white paper describing the *Money Catcher Strategy*. Our focus here will be to break down the strategy to its fundamental building blocks. We then will reconstruct the operational methodology with modifications to enhance its efficacy for maximum performance."

"The *Butterfly Option Combination* is an assemblage of two *Option Spreads*, a *Bullish Debit Spread* with a *Bearish Credit Spread*. Both *Spreads* share a common middle-leg *strike price*. Each *Spread* is formed from the simultaneous purchase and sale of *options* associated with the same underlying asset at differing *strike prices* and having the same *expiration date*."

"As confusing as that sounds now, it will become second nature to you with practice. It is a simple idea once understood, so please give it a chance."

"Can anyone tell me what an an *option* is?" Dr. Nelson asked.

"Well in terms of stock," One of the participants answered. "It is a contract to buy or sell 100 shares of the underlying stock, or the stock that the *option* is associated with, at a specified price, on or before a specified date."

"Correct." Dr. Nelson continued. "The specified price is the *strike price*, and the specified date is the *expiration date*."

"*Options* come in two basic denominations, *calls* and *puts. Calls* are contracts to buy shares of the underlying asset. *Puts* are contracts to sell shares of the underlying asset."

"So a *call option* buyer is purchasing a contract giving him or her the right to buy 100 shares of the underlying stock at a given price on or before a certain date, after which that right no longer exists. It, in fact, has *expired*." Dr. Nelson explained.

"*Options* are offered in a series of *strike prices*. If the underlying asset, which we will call stock XYZ, presently is trading at $50 per share, then *options* associated with the $50 *strike price* are *at-the-money*. *Call options* offered at *strike prices* below $50 are *in-the-money*, and *call options* offered at *strike prices* above $50 are *out-of-the-money*.

"*Put options* offered at strike prices below $50 are *out-of-the-money*, and *put options* offered at strike prices above $50 are *in-the-money*."

"Depending on *strike price* position relative to the the *at-the-money* underlying asset price, *options* have *intrinsic value* and/or *time value*. *In-the-money options* have *intrinsic value*, while *at-the-money* and *out-of-the-money options* have no *intrinsic value*. *Intrinsic value* represents the value of the *option* at *expiration*. So a $40 *strike call option* has an *intrinsic value* of $10 when the XYZ stock is priced at $50. Similarly, a $60 *strike put option* has an *intrinsic value* of $10 since it is $10 *in-the-money*."

"All options have *time value* until they *expire*. *Time value* measures the lifespan of the *option* until *expiration*. *Options* with longer lifespans have higher *time value* than *options* with shorter lifespans. *Time value* decreases as *options* approach *expiration*, and the decrease accelerates as the *expiration* gets closer."

"A $40 *strike* XYZ *call option* which can be bought for $12, then would have $10 of *intrinsic value* and $2 of *time value*. A $60 *strike* XYZ *call* offered at $2 would be entirely made up of *time value*."

"Conversely, a $60 *strike* XYZ *put option* which can be bought for

$12, then would have $10 of *intrinsic value* and $2 of *time value*. A $40 *strike* XYZ *put* offered at $2 would be entirely made up of *time value*."

"Both *calls* and *puts* can be bought and/or sold. One is not obligated to hold contracts until *expiration*."

"Can anyone suggest why one might want to purchase or sell an *option*." Dr. Nelson asked.

"Leverage." A participant answered.

"Good." Dr. Nelson replied. "*Options* provide leverage which can increase profitability. It can also work to one's disadvantage."

"Consider our $50 XYZ stock. One can purchase the $40 *strike call option* for $12. Then if XYZ rises in price to say $55, the *option* will have a new value of about $17 with $15 of *intrinsic value*. That represents an increase of nearly 42%, while the XYZ stock increase is merely 10%."

"Recall that each *option* contract represents 100 shares of the underlying stock. The $12 *call option* then would cost $1,200 to purchase. To purchase 100 shares of XYZ stock outright one must cough up $5,000, or around four times the *option* cost. Said another way, one can *control* 100 shares of XYZ for about one quarter the price through the purchase of a *call option*."

"Should the price of XYZ drop to $45, the *call* owner would experience a loss of nearly 42% with the *call option* now having only $5 of intrinsic value.

"Weren't *options* created to provide insurance for stockholders?" A second participant asked.

"Indeed they were." Dr. Nelson responded. "And the insurance can be applied to ensuring price valuation when stock shares are purchased and when stock shares are sold. For a small premium above the present *at-the-money* stock value, one can fix the purchase price for 100 shares of XYZ stock through the purchase of an *at-the-money call option*. That purchase price is effective until the *call option expires*. Conversely, a stock holder can fix the sale price for 100 shares of XYZ until *expiration* through the purchase of an *at-the-money put option*."

"The primary drawbacks for owning *options* are *time value* degradation and eventual *expiration*. Every day an *option* is owned, its *time-value* component decreases. Any *option* expiring *out-of-the-money* will expire without value. Further *out-of-the-money options* are not likely to be exercised, or converted into underlying stock shares. The *option* owner would not buy shares at a price higher than the open market price of those shares, nor sell shares at a price lower than the open market share price. All *options* expiring *in-the-money* or *at-the-money* are automatically exercised during settlement. This can result in a margin call if insufficient funds exist in the brokerage account to execute the required purchase, or if insufficient shares exist to execute the required sale."

"We will now take a break and let these ideas sink in." Dr. Nelson said in conclusion. "In our next session, we will focus on combining the purchase and sale of *options* to create *spreads* and *combinations*."

CHAPTER 9

As Dr. Nelson continued with The Patriot Project training, word came down that Congress had approved Condition 5 and had sent legislation to President Cotton for his signature. According to Condition 5, 'There shall be no enactment of laws extending beyond the active congressional term. No bills shall be passed or signed unread and not duly deliberated.' This was a huge step for the Legislative Branch toward renewing its purpose and limiting its evolving overreach. Approval polls began showing immediate improvement in public sentiment toward overall government function and the direction in which the country was headed.

Congress still struggled with Condition 6 which would abolish the income tax code and replace it with a flat consumption tax. This was not surprising, but at least the topic was being discussed seriously for the first time ever, a long overdue event.

"*Options* may be purchased and *options* may be sold." Dr. Nelson began, addressing the next Patriot Project training session. "The consequences of each action are considerably different. Recall that *option* buyers have the *right*, but not the *obligation*, to purchase or sell 100 shares of underlying asset at a specified *strike price* on or before a specified *expiration date*. Hence option buyers are in control of the decision to exercise or assign the purchase or sale of underlying asset shares until *expiration*. Option buyers pay a premium for owning this right."

"Option sellers are *obligated* to purchase or sell 100 shares of underlying asset whenever the *options* sold are exercised or assigned. *Call option* sellers are obligated to deliver shares, and *put option* sellers are obligated to purchase shares. *Option* sellers are compensated for assuming that obligation. They, in fact, have the premium that *option* buyers pay added to their account upon executing the *option* sale. This makes *option* selling a potential income source for astute risk takers."

"Consider our XYZ stock which presently sells for $50 per share. One might purchase a 50-*strike call option* expiring on September 15 for $2 and own the right to purchase 100 share at $50 per share until *expiration*. Alternatively, one might sell the same 50-*strike call option* and collect $2. If we assume that September 15 is one month away, that $2 represents a gain of 4% relative to the $50 strike price for a one month holding period. Should one do this every month of the year, that would represent an annual return of 48%."

"This income does not reflect price movement of the underlying XYZ stock. It does not reflect losses or gains associated with having the *call option* assigned. It merely represents opportunity income available to qualified traders."

"In our example above, no mention is made of owning the underlying asset in association with selling the *call option*. When a trader sells a *call option* without ownership of at least 100 shares of the underlying asset, that trade, or position, is said to be *naked*. Should the call be assigned, the option seller will have to purchase shares of XYZ on the open exchange at the current market price to complete the delivery."

"Should the call seller own 100 shares of XYZ in his or her trading account and have that *call option* assigned, then those 100 XYZ shares will be transferred to the *option* owner exercising the right. The *call* will *expire* and the *option* seller will receive payment of 100 times the $50 strike-price, or $5,000. The $200 collected when selling the *call* originally will remain in the *option* seller's account. When a trader sells a *call option* and owns at least 100 shares of the underlying asset, that trade, or position, is said to be *covered*."

"*Put options* also can be traded *naked* or *covered*. Here the *put* seller would necessarily hold a *short* position of 100 XYZ shares to establish coverage. Upon assignment the *put* seller would purchase 100 XYZ shares at the $50 strike-price. Again the seller collects the *option* premium for assuming the *obligation* of completing the assignment transaction."

"In general, *option* buyers are hoping the *option* purchased finishes or expires *in-the-money* with a positive *intrinsic value*. *Option* sellers are hoping the *option* sold finishes or expires *out-of-the-money* with zero *time value*."

"And now before we continue on with our introduction to *option spreads*, can anyone explain what a *bid-ask spread* is?" Dr. Nelson inquired.

"The difference between the *best bid*, or buy price offered and the *best ask*, or sell price offered" A session participant offered confidently.

"That is correct, and a good synopsis of an open market transaction." Dr. Nelson responded. "If a trader submits a m*arket order* to *purchase* shares or contracts of an asset on an open market exchange, that order will be filled immediately at the present *ask price*. This is the lowest price presently offered among traders actively seeking to sell this asset."

"If a trader submits a *market order* to *sell* shares or contracts of an asset on an open market exchange, that order will be filled immediately at the present *bid price*. This is the highest price presently offered among traders actively seeking to buy this asset."

"The *ask price* is always higher than the *bid price*, but the distance between the *bid* and *ask prices* can vary. This distance is called the *bid-ask spread*."

"The *bid-ask spread* always works to the disadvantage of the retail trader." Dr. Nelson continued. "One must overcome the difference between the *bid* and *ask* prices before any profit can be realized on a trade, and that is before transaction commissions and fees are assessed. The *bid-ask spread* serves as compensation for the market maker for the risks that he or she assumes attempting to match buy and sell orders."

"In general, a narrow *bid-ask spread* usually is associated with heavily traded stocks, ETFs which are exchange-traded funds, and/or *options*. It indicates a condition of high liquidity, or low friction, which results in easy entry and exit from traded positions."

"A wide *bid-ask spread* usually is associated with thinly traded stocks, ETFs, and/or *options*. It indicates a condition of low liquidity, or high friction, which results in difficult entry and exit from traded positions."

"The *bid-ask spread* can be thought of as the *trade-negotiation zone*. The narrower the zone, the better the chances for obtaining order fills, but the smaller the profit potential. Conversely, the wider the zone, the lesser the chance for obtaining order fills, but the greater the profit potential."

"One more important consideration, before we dive into the topic of *option spread* trading. Recall that *option* sellers assume considerable risk for the relatively small income earned. There are in fact three sources of risk: *early-assignment risk*, *dividend risk* and *interest-rate risk* events.

"When an *option* buyer decides to exercise his or her *option*, the *option* seller assigned becomes *obligated* to complete the transaction. If a *call option* is sold and later assigned or exercised by the buyer, the seller is *obligated* to deliver 100 shares of the underlying stock on demand. If a *put option* is sold and later assigned or exercised by the buyer, the seller is obligated to purchase 100 shares of the underlying stock from the buyer on demand. The assignment process is automatic and random and may not affect all *option* sellers."

"Upon assignment, the shares of underlying stock obligated either enters (per *put* sold) or exits (per *call* sold) one's account. If insufficient funds are available to execute the required transaction, the account owner will receive a *margin call*. The broker will notify the account owner of the assignment and request that additional funds be added to the account to complete transaction execution. If the additional funds are unavailable, the broker will likely complete the obligated transaction via loaned funds, or *margin*. An interest charge will be issued for as long as the loan remains in effect, a minimum of one day. The interest rate charged is subject to the whims of the market, either increasing or decreasing, and may impact option sellers favorably or unfavorably. Therefore, *interest rate risk* is among the *obligations* assumed by *option* sellers."

"Should the underlying asset for the *option* sold pay a dividend, the *option* seller assumes additional risk when that position is held through the ex-dividend date. When a stock goes ex-dividend, anyone owning shares of that stock becomes entitled to received the declared dividend payment. Anyone who is *short* that stock, having sold shares in anticipation of a price decline, will be charged an amount equal to the dividend payment per share at ex-dividend. The owner of a *call option* for a dividend-paying stock can exercise that *call* prior to the ex-dividend date to qualify for receiving the dividend payment. This early-assignment transaction could create a *short* stock position in the *option* seller's account and result in an associated dividend-payment deduction."

"*Dividend risk* can be reduced by avoiding *short-call* positions for dividend-paying stocks. It cannot be eliminated entirely for *short-calls* on stocks, because any company can declare a special dividend unexpectedly. Careful monitoring of the underlying stock should be practiced when writing *calls*."

"To recap," Dr. Nelson summarized. "*Option* writers or sellers are subject to three sources of risk that are not of particular concern to *option* buyers. These are *early assignment risk, dividend risk,* and *interest rate risk. Option* buyers, however, are impacted by *expiration* assignment for *in-the-money* and *at-the-money options,* as are *option* sellers. These risks are greatly reduced for *covered option* trades in comparison to *naked option* trades."

"It should be noted that approximately 90% of *options* traded are never exercised by the *option* owner. This indicates that *options* probably are used mostly for speculation. More importantly, it suggests that *option* selling might be less risky than it appears at first glance. *Option* traders however should be aware that the risks are ever present, and accordingly ensure that *short options,* especially *uncovered* ones, are positioned *out-of-the-money*."

"The trouble most *option* traders encounter usually stems from over-leveraging. Since *options* are priced cheap relative to actual asset ownership, there is a big temptation to over purchase or over sell the positions in an attempt to accelerate gains. When this backfires, the result is accelerated losses."

"It should be noted," Dr. Nelson continued. "that there are two classes of options: *American Style* and *European Style. American Style options* can be exercised on any day of the active life of the *option* up until *expiration. European Style options* can be exercised only on the last day before *option expiration*. Most securities traded on the major exchanges are *American Style*. Several heavily-traded cash-settled index securities are *European Style*."

"That finally brings us to the topic of *option spreads,* which we will consider in detail immediately following the break." Dr. Nelson concluded.

CHAPTER 10

"During this session, we will consider the topic of *option spreads.*" Dr. Nelson began. "An *option spread* is created when one simultaneously purchases and sells two related *options*. The *options* bought and sold must be associated with the same underlying asset. Other than that the variations are nearly endless. Our focus will be on *vertical spreads,* since these are the ones that are most useful in constructing the *Money Catcher Strategy.*"

"*Vertical spreads* incorporate the buying and sell of *options* of the same type, either both *calls* or both *puts*. These *options* are associated with the same underlying stock, or asset, and also have the same *expiration date*. The *option* bought differs from the *option* sold because the buying and selling take place at differing *strike prices.*"

"*Vertical spreads* are the simplest form of *option combination*. Understanding the risks and rewards of *verticals spreads* will help to demonstrate the powerful possibilities and protections that come with combining more than one *option* contract in a single trade order. Just as two or more *options* can be used to construct a *vertical spread,* two or more *vertical spreads* can be used to construct *higher order combinations*. This can be advantageous almost beyond comprehension. So let's look at *vertical spreads* a little closer."

"There are four *vertical spreads*: Two are *bullish*, meaning they tend to make money when the price of the underlying asset increases. Two are *bearish*, meaning they tend to make money when the price of the underlying asset decreases."

"Number one is the *vertical debit call spread* which is *bullish*. The *vertical debit call spread* is constructed from buying a *lower strike call* and selling a *higher strike call*, and can make money if the underlying stock rises in price, and also if the stock price remains stable, as long as both *calls* finish or *expire in-the-money*. If the stock price moves down, and both *calls expire out-of-the-money,* the *spread* position will lose money."

"Number two is the *vertical credit call spread* which is *bearish*. The *vertical credit call spread is* constructed from buying a *higher strike call* and selling a *lower strike call,* and can make money if the underlying stock drops in price, and also if the stock price remains stable, as long as both *calls* finish or *expire out-of-the-money.* If the stock price moves higher, and both *calls expire in-the-money*, the *spread* position will lose money."

"Number three is the *vertical debit put spread* which is *bearish.* The *vertical debit put spread* is constructed from buying a *higher strike put* and selling a *lower strike put* can make money if the underlying stock drops in price, and also if the stock price remains stable, as long as both *puts* finish or *expire in-the-money.* If the stock price moves higher, and both *puts expire out-of-the-money,* the *spread* position will lose money."

"Number four is the *vertical credit put spread* which is *bullish*. The *vertical credit put spread* is constructed from buying a *lower strike put* and selling a *higher strike put,* and can make money if the underlying stock rises in price, and also if the stock price remains stable, as long as both *puts* finish or *out-of-the-money.* If the stock price moves lower, and both *puts expire* in-the-money, the *spread* position will lose money."

"Vertical spreads take advantage of both directional movements and *time-value* decay. Compared to *naked call* and *put options*, *vertical spread* trading offers limited risk in exchange for limited reward. *Vertical spreads* also offer a more efficient use of buying power. They are cheaper to purchase than *naked options*."

"Let's look at an example. Stock XYZ is presently trading at $50 and *call options* at the 45 *strike* are priced at $6.00 while *call options* at the 50 *strike* are priced at $3.00. One could purchase a 45 *strike call* and pay $600 per contract. Recall that each contract represents 100 shares of the underlying stock or asset, or XYZ Stock in this case. This would give the buyer the opportunity for unlimited upside profit potential for the $600 at risk. Alternatively, one could purchase a 45/50 *vertical debit call spread* for $300 and control the same 100 shares of XYZ Stock. A $300 *credit* for the 50-strike *call option* sold minus a $600 *debit* for the 45-strike *call option* purchased to create this spread equals a $300 overall *debit*. The 45-*strike call* buy and 50-*strike call* sell can be entered simultaneously on an order entry ticket."

"Note here that the maximum profit for the *vertical spread* is $500, which is the difference between the 50 and 45 *strikes*, or $5 multiplied by 100 shares per contract. This $500 divided by $300 at risk equals a 66.7% gain when fully realized. This limited profit can be realized if the underlying stock increases in price, or even if XYZ remains at its current price of $50.00. The price of XYZ can decrease for an amount of up to $2.00 before the *spread* is no longer profitable."

"The 45-*strike naked call* usually will require the underlying asset to increase a sufficient amount before *expiration* to yield a profit. If the underlying asset remains unchanged in price, the *call option* will lose $100 in time value by *expiration*. And of course, if the underlying stock decreases in value, the *naked call* will lose value by a proportionate amount by *expiration*. If XYZ Stock closes below $45 at *expiration*, the 45-*strike naked call* will expire worthless and *out-of-the-money*."

"For half of the cost of an *in-the-money naked call option* here, one can enter an *in-the-money vertical-debit-call spread* with a limited profit potential, but with a greater chance of having that profit realized."

"*Debit vertical spreads* are usually positioned slightly *in-the-money*. They are most profitable when both options expire *in-the-money*. *Credit vertical spreads* are usually positioned slightly *out-of-the-money*. They are most profitable when both options expire *out-of-the-money*."

"One does not have to hold *vertical spreads* until they expire. One can sell or buy back *vertical spreads* at any time prior to *expiration*. Any time a sufficient profit is realized is a good time to consider exiting a *vertical spread* position. Further, one is only limited by the *option* buying power in ones trading account as to how many *vertical spreads* one may purchase or sell."

"Under certain unique circumstances, which will be discussed further a little later, *debit vertical spreads* can be purchased for a *credit*. Imagine purchasing a *debit vertical spread* and getting paid to do so! That is risk-free trading profit when the position is closed out or sold before *option expiration*."

"Please note here that my Think-or-Swim app *will not accept* a *vertical-debit-spread* limit-buy order for a negative value (which essentially is the same as asking for a *credit*) as a valid trade order. Think-or-Swim, however, *will accept* a *vertical-debit-spread* limit-buy order for a value of $0. Bidding to buy a *vertical spread* for $0 and getting filled at a better price than offered accomplishes the same objective, and appears to work."

"So in summary, *options* do not have to be held onto until they reach *expiration*. *Long options* can be sold and *short options* bought at any time before *option expiration* to close owned or obligated positions. Upon closure, a profit, or loss, or no value change will be realized with one's account adjusted accordingly, and no further trade risks will be assumed. *Vertical spreads* individually can be bought and sold for profit just easily as *naked options*. *Vertical spreads* also can be combined to produce more favorable profit profiles. *Butterfly Combinations, Condor Combinations, Box Spreads,* and other advanced *Spread* trades each are composed from adding together two or more differing *Vertical Spreads*. The resulting *combination* trade can be designed to be non-directional, where a profit can be made regardless of directional price movement of the underlying stock or asset. Since prediction of stock movement is difficult particularly over the short term, non-directional strategies just might turn out to be a more profitable trading approach."

"In our next session, we will focus on the *Butterfly Combination*. I realize that this might seem to be a considerable amount of technical detail to digest right now. But hang in there, soon you will see how this all fits together. The *Butterfly Combination* has some pretty amazing properties, which I believe you will find as fascinating and profitable as I have discovered."

CHAPTER 11

It is truly astonishing what can be accomplished when one's back is against the wall. Perceiving no other way out, and refusing to descend further with a sinking ship, Congress passed legislation addressing Condition 6. The income tax code was officially abolished and replaced with a simplified flat consumption tax. Had things not progressed to the point that they had, this act alone might have gone far toward restoring The United States to glory. Now it was up to Dr. Nelson and the Patriot Project to come through.

"Welcome to the *Butterfly* session!" Dr. Nelson began, smiling and gesturing. "Here is where the rubber meets the road. If you are not amazed by what we are about to cover, then you might not be alive!"

"Briefly, a *butterfly option trade* is a combined *debit-spread/credit-spread* three-legged trade using either all *call options* or all *put options* for all three legs. The *options* are transacted at three different *strike prices* (the legs). Most commonly one *option* is bought at an *in-the-money strike price*, two *options* are sold at or near the *at-the-money strike price*, and the remaining option is bought at an *out-of-the-money strike price*. This creates a *long butterfly combination*. The distance between *strike prices* are equal, and weekly or monthly *options* may be used. Usually the closer to *option expiration*, the more responsive the *option prices* to movements in the underlying security."

"Think of this as an A-B-C trade, where one A and one C are bought and two Bs are sold. An order to buy one (A-2B+C) ratio *combination* is place with your broker on a single trade ticket."

"Let's return to our example." Dr. Nelson continued. "Recall that XYZ stock is presently priced at $50 per share. *Call options* for the September 15 *expiration* are priced at $6 for the 45 *strike*, $3 for the 50 *strike*, and $1 for the 55 *strike*. If we sell two 50-*strike calls* and purchase one 45-*strike call* and purchase one 55-*strike call*, the *long butterfly combination* created will cost us $100. The purchase equation looks like ((2x$3)-$6-$1) x 100 = -$100."

Dr. Nelson scribbled the numbers and letters on a white board positioned on an easel in front of the seated participants.

"The *long call butterfly combination* is market neutral." Dr. Nelson continued. It can make money if XYZ increases in price by *expiration*, decreases in price by *expiration*, or remains unchanged by *expiration*. If the XYZ price increases too much, which in this case means beyond $54, the *upper break-even price*, the position will lose money. If the XYZ price decreases too much, which in this case means below $46, the *lower break-even price*, the position will lose money. The maximum amount that this position can lose is the $100 original entry cost at risk."

"Should the XYZ price finish between the *lower* and *upper break-even prices* at *expiration*, the *butterfly* position will be profitable with maximum profitability attained at the $50 *strike-price*. The maximum profit, minus commissions and fees, is $400, which is the value of the $5 *vertical spread* finishing entirely *in-the-money* times 100 shares minus the $100 original entry cost. That is a 400% return on the $100 at risk."

"*Butterfly combination* traders anticipate little to no price movement in the underlying asset between trade onset and *expiration*. But there can be additional advantages. Consider that the cost of ownership of 100 shares of XYZ is $5,000 plus fees. Recall that the cost of the *in-the-money* 45-*strike call* controlling 100 XYZ shares is $600 plus fees. The cost of an *in-the-money vertical debit spread* controlling 100 shares of XYZ is $300 plus fees. The *butterfly combination* controlling 100 XYZ shares is only $100 plus fees. Hence, the money at risk for control of the same 100 shares of XYZ is less."

"The *butterfly combination* is a *covered option* trade, which reduces risk. In fact, the *butterfly combination* is an ideal candidate for day trading for reasons we will now explore."

"The profit expectation chart for the *long butterfly combination* at *expiration* is fixed, and is composed of four straight lines. Line number one is horizontal and extends from the $0 price to the *in-the-money option strike-price*, or $45 in our continuing example. The line is valued at -$100 on the Y-axis, which is the at risk entry price. Line number two is diagonal and increases on the Y-axis from -$100 at the 45 *in-the-money strike* to $400 at the 50 *at-the-money strike*. Line number three is diagonal and decreases on the Y-axis from $400 at the 50 *at-the-money strike* to -$100 at the 55 *out-of-the-money strike*. Line number four is horizontal and extends from the 55 *out-of-the-money strike* to infinity at a value of -$100."

"The maximum profitability is rarely ever achieved with the *butterfly combination.* So it makes sense to exit the trade whenever a decent level of profit is attained. And here is where things begin to get interesting. While the profit expectation lines for the *option expiration* date remain fixed, there can be considerable movement and distortion to the shape of the profit expectation line on trading days leading up to *expiration* when the markets are open. Said another way, when the stock markets are open, the profit expectation line on simple pictorial charts *move* as the market price of the underlying asset fluctuates."

"Imagine a hump shaped line where the profit zone is the area beneath the hump. This line moves up and down while the hump expands and contracts...enough so that a small profit can be realized from well-timed and carefully-positioned buy and sell trades.

"The interaction of individual *option* prices when combined during active trading results in both horizontal and vertical price movements
of the quoted butterfly combination price. Said another way, the quoted *bid-ask spread* widens when more *options* are incorporated into the *combination* buy order. The *trade-negotiation zone* between the buyer and seller widens leading to larger potential profits."

"Let's say one places a buy order that is filled for a $1.00 *debit*. Immediately thereafter one might place a sell order for $1.20 *credit*. A sell order is the mirror image of the buy order, where one A *option* and one C *option* are now sold and the two B *options* are bought back (which creates a *short butterfly combination*). Ideally, this will result in a round-trip day trade which yields a $0.20 profit after the trade settles."

"While $0.20 doesn't sound like a lot, understand that multiple *butterfly combinations* can be traded. For example, one can place an order to buy 5, 10, 20, 50, 100, or more *combinations*. Hence, upon selling potentially, one can collect $1.00, $2.00, $4.00, $10.00, or $20.00 or more per *round-trip* trade. As you might recall, each *option* contract represents 100 shares of the underlying security. Thus one may actually collect $100, $200, $400, $1,000, $2,000, or more per *round-trip* trade. Imagine turning over five or ten successful *round-trip* trades in a single trading day with each producing a few hundred or a few thousand dollars!"

"As exciting as that sounds," Dr. Nelson continued. "It gets better."

"The big secret that no one appears to be telling anyone is that one should choose *strike prices* that are as close together as possible. If the underlying security is trading *options* at $1 *strike-price* intervals, the buy and sell prices of the (A-2B+C) *options* should be transacted $1 apart. The B *options* commonly are sold as close to the present price of the underlying security as possible. So with the underlying trading at say $50, one might purchase *options* at the $49 and $51 *strikes* and sell twice as many $50 *strike options.* This results in a *Skinny Butterfly Combination.*"

"The advantage of this approach may not appear immediately evident. At first glance, it appears counter intuitive and destined for certain failure. With market prices being so dynamic and fluid (not to mention random) during trading hours, how can one possibly expect for the trade to remain in the extremely-narrow *profit zone* long enough to earn a profit? The surprising answer is that *it doesn't have to.* Prices bounce around throughout the day as orders are executed by various market makers. All one has to do is be close to the trading price of the underlying security to make this work."

"Not only is the *bid-ask spread* wider when *higher-order combinations* are traded, but the quoted *bid price* often becomes negative. This suggests that *long* or *debit combinations* might be purchased for a *credit* if one is patient. I have had considerable success at employing limit-orders to buy *higher-order combinations* bidding $0 debit. These usually are filled for a *credit*, sometimes a substantial one. Conversely, I have closed these positions asking $0 *credit* and received sizable *credits* beyond my *ask*. This might sound too good to be believed, but consider the size of "wiggle room" between the quoted *bid* and *ask* prices. One can enter a trade position for a *credit*, a *debit*, or at no cost, and still have plenty of room to capture a profit."

"And now after a short intermission,"Dr. Nelson concluded. "We will further our adventure with the amazing *Skinny Butterfly Combination* trade. See you soon."

CHAPTER 12

"I first discovered the power of the *Skinny Butterfly* trade when experimenting with AMZN stock. AMZN is the ticker symbol of stock shares for the retail giant Amazon.com." Dr. Nelson opened. "I was trying to emulate the exchange market makers initially, because they seem to be successful at matching buy and sell orders while earning a small profit on every trade they execute. I was thinking perhaps if I could day-trade in and out of a market security a multitude of times, simply taking relatively small profits along the way, without getting burned, then that approach might be workable."

"I chose AMZN as the underlying asset for my *option* positions, because it was a very actively traded stock. The individual *options* for AMZN therefore had relatively narrow *bid-ask spreads* making it easy to enter and exit positions. AMZN was relatively expensive to own as well. Trading at approximately $1,500 per share, purchasing 100 shares required an outlay of $150,000!"

"The *at-the-money call options* for AMZN for the closest expiration traded between a $50 *bid* and a $55 *ask,* which was about 3% of the underlying price. The *at-the-money long skinny butterfly-combinations* traded between a -$3.50 *bid* and a $4.25 *ask,* which was about 0.3% of the underlying price."

"Did you catch the point that the *bid-ask* negotiation zone for the *long skinny butterfly combinations* was significantly wider than for individual *call options*? Did you notice that the range of that zone dipped significantly into *negative* territory? How might one capitalize on this situation?"

After a brief pause for dramatic emphasis, Dr. Nelson continued.

"The answer turns out to be relatively simple. One enters and exits trade positions using *limit orders*. If I wish to buy a *long* AMZN *butterfly combination*, I fill in the *strike-price* values, *expiration date* value, and *minimum* buy price I will accept as a *limit-buy order*. If my order executes, I will become owner of the position at the buy price I specify, *or better*. So what buy price is acceptable?"

"Noticing that a portion of the *bid-ask spread* is *negative*, I might attempt to enter a *negative* value for my *limit buy* price. Could this be possible?"

"Understand what I am suggesting here. A *negative* value for a buy order results in a *credit*! That means money is added to my account for the privilege of owning a *long skinny* AMZN *butterfly combination.* This is like walking into a grocery store and buying a quart of milk. When I reach the checkout counter, the clerk bags my purchase and hands me a couple of bucks! I can then turn around and sell that quart of milk to someone else and collect another couple of bucks!"

"What I have discovered is that Think-or Swim will indeed accept *negative bids*, or buy-price requests as *limit orders* for *long combinations*. Think-or-Swim will *not* accept *negative bids* for *vertical debit spreads*. They *will* accept a \$0 *bid* for *vertical debit spreads*. Further, it is possible to enter a \$0 *bid* and have it filled for a *credit*, which accomplishes the same objective."

"I will give you a moment or two to digest this. Then we will look at an example."

After another brief pause, Dr. Nelson continued.

"With AMZN trading at \$1,500 per share, one might submit a *limit-buy order* to purchase the *at-the-money long call butterfly* for the closest *expiration* and *bid* -\$0.10 to fill. Here, on one order ticket, the broker is instructed to buy one 1495-*strike call*, sell two 1500-*strike calls*, and buy one 1505-*strike call* simultaneously for the -\$0.10 price or better. Should this order fill, then one's account is credited with $10 or more plus the position. This is more than enough to cover the commission, which is the cost of putting on the trade, in this case $2.60. The effect on the account *buying power* is $0. After commission is deducted, the account is *credited* with $7.40."

"Because there is *no negative buying power effect*, theoretically one can order as many *butterfly combinations* as one might wish. In the real world, there are limitations. The Think-or-Swim brokerage trade ticket permits up to 99,998 *combinations* per order. So a single fully-loaded order ticket when filled would yield $7.40 x 99,998 or $739,985.20 at the minimum. Not a bad return for very little effort."

"Further, one can submit as many orders as one can create with *no negative buying power effect*."

"One can then turn around and sell the *butterfly combinations* bought for further profit. Once one qualifies for day-trading options, this turnaround or *round-trip* trade can be completed in a matter of minutes or seconds. Buying for -$0.10 and selling for $0.20 yields a
minimum of $24.80 per *butterfly round-trip* trade, which translates to $2,479,950.40 minimum per *round-trip* for a fully-loaded order ticket."

"One can request more on both sides of the trade, but experience has taught me that the further from $0 one ventures, the longer it takes to realize order fills, if they fill at all."

It is of particular interest that AMZN *butterfly-combination* trades do *not* have to be centered on the *at-the-money* price. One can position *skinny butterflies* a hundred or more dollars *out-of-the-money* and still have them successfully fill. One can position *skinny butterflies* farther from the *expiration date* and have them successfully fill. Generally speaking the farther away from the *at-the-money* price, both horizontally (via price separation) and vertically (via *time-value* increase), the less active *options* will trade. The safer *option* positions are from exposure to assignment risks, the longer they take to execute."

"We have discussed the risks associated with *short option* positions. With highly leveraged positions, unexpected *options exercise* can result in devastating loss if the market moves against the asset position created via assignment. While AMZN is a tremendous underlying stock to focus on for trading *skinny butterfly combinations*, such trades do not come without risk. Since *long butterfly combinations* contain *short options*, there is always a possibility that those *short options* get exercised or assigned. And even though the *butterfly combination* is a *covered* trade, realized ownership or delivery *obligation* of AMZN shares can result in a greater cost or reward than the original *option combination* position would have yielded. AMZN stock options are *American Style options* which are subject to early assignment."

"To avoid assignment risk before *expiration*, I looked to assets offering European Style options. To make a long story short, I discovered only two that had the characteristics required to make the *Money Catcher Strategy* successful, SPX and NDX. Both SPX and NDX are high priced assets, and both are very heavily traded on the open exchanges."

"SPX is the ticker symbol for the Standard and Poor's 500 Index, a stock index representing the 500 largest companies with shares listed on NYSE (the New York Stock Exchange) or NASDAQ (the National Association of Securities Dealers Automated Quotations exchange). SPX is priced around $3,000 and is very heavily traded. *Options* for SPX are among the most liquid of all *options* offered for trading. SPX *options* are cash-settled *European Style options*, which can be exercised only on the last day before *expiration*."

"NDX is the ticker symbol for an exchange-traded index fund representing the 100 largest non-financial companies listed on the NASDAQ stock market. NDX is priced around $12,000 which is approximately four times greater than the price of SPX shares. NDX *options* reflect NDX price movements in an extremely exaggerated fashion, which works well with the *Money Catcher Strategy*. Additionally, NDX *options* are cash-settled European Style options which can be exercised only on the last day before *expiration*."

"With SPX and NDX, we have the potential to implement risk-free trades. When the *long skinny butterfly combinations* are entered for a *credit* using *options* associated with SPX or NDX, one can safely hold these positions through *expiration*. At *expiration*, all *options* are converted to their expiring cash value with no underlying asset ownership or delivery *obligations*. This could well result in additional profit. But why wait until *expiration* to close out a position when you can complete the *round-trip* trade as soon as the position is created?"

"With both SPX and NDX, *options* are available at *strike prices* spaced at $5.00 intervals. Such closely spaced *option strikes* relative to the price of the underlying asset creates frequent attractive *Arbitrage* opportunities as *option* prices fluctuate during active trading. This means that *bid-ask spreads* for adjacent *options* momentarily overlap during open market trading sessions, creating situations where *long option combinations* can be purchased for a *credit*. As stated earlier, one can capture these *credit* opportunities using *limit-buy orders*."

"Our next session will take us to our ultimate goal - the *Balanced-Skewed Skinny-Butterfly Combination* – which will be the work horse for generating trillion-dollar returns."

CHAPTER 13

"To recap our journey so far," Dr. Nelson began. "We began with a discussion of *Options* and underlying assets. From there we considered combining differing but related *Options* to form *Spreads, Vertical Spreads* in particular. We then discussed combining *Vertical Spreads* to form *Option Combinations, Butterfly Combinations* in particular, and then focused on *Skinny-Butterfly Combinations*. We then considered the advantages of using cash-settled *European Style Options* associated with underlying market equity index assets. Our focus today will be on enhancing the *Money Catcher* to obtain maximum performance."

"*Butterfly combinations* do not have to be *balanced*. They can be *skewed* in a number of ways to achieve more favorable profit profiles. There is the *Broken-wing Butterfly Combination* and the *Unbalanced Butterfly Combination*, both of which seek to capitalize on some directional movement bias in the underlying asset. Researching these has led to the discovery of something I will term the *Balanced-Skewed Skinny-Butterfly Combination*, which will be our focus here."

"Recall that a *long skinny butterfly* is created when one A-*strike option* is purchased, two B-*strike options* are sold, and one C-*strike option* is purchased. This is a three-strike-price *combination* formed from uniting a b*ull-debit-vertical spread* with b*ear-credit-vertical spread*. Here, all *options* are of the same type (either *call* or *put*), and all are associated with the same underlying asset or stock, and all have the same *expiration* date. Further, the A-*strike*, B-*strike*, and C-*strike options* are adjacent *strike options*, and the spacing between adjacent *strike options* is equidistant. This *butterfly combination* is *balanced* because the *long* A-*strike* and *long* C-*strike options* are spaced equidistant from the *short* B-*strike options*. Said another way, a *long vertical-debit spread* is paired with a *short vertical-credit spread*, and both share the same *short-option strike* price. In addition, one can buy and sell more than one *butterfly combination* on a trade-order ticket. So one can trade a single *butterfly combination*," Dr. Nelson scribbled '(1A-2B+1C)' on his white board. "Or multiple *butterfly combinations*. For example," He scribbled '(2A-4B+2C)', or '(3A-6B+3C)', or '(10A-20B+10C).'

"If one were to purchase one A-*strike option*, sell two B-*strike options*, skip over the C-*strike* and also purchase one D-*strike option*, then one would have created a *broken-wing butterfly* with a bear*ish* bias. To *re-balance* the *butterfly*, one might purchase an additional A-*strike option* and simultaneously sell an additional B-*strike option*. This results in a (2A-3B+1D) *balanced-skewed skinny-butterfly combination*, which yields more powerful price movements than a simple (1A-2B+1C) *balanced* skinny-*butterfly combination*. The (2A-3B+1D) *balanced-skewed skinny-butterfly combination* incorporates a greater number of *option* contracts than the simple (1A-2B+1C) b*alanced-skinny-butterfly combination*, which partially at least might explain the greater price volatility."

"Notice that b*roken-wing butterfly* is *skewed*. That is, the *long D-strike option* is spaced twice the distance from the *short B-strike options* than the *long A-strike option*. Purchasing an additional (A-D)-*strike vertical-debit spread* re-balances the b*utterfly*, but the *combination* remains somewhat *skewed*. If the D-*strike* price is positioned $10.00 above the B-*strike* price, then the A-*strike* price is positioned $5.00 below the B-*strike* price. It takes two (A-B)-*strike vertical-debit spreads* to balance one (B+D)-*strike vertical-credit spread*." Dr. Nelson scribbled the equation '(2 x $5.00 = $10.00)' on the board.

"One can stretch out the *butterfly* over a number of *strike* prices. For example, one might enter a (3A-4B+1E) *butterfly* , or a (4A-5B +1F) *butterfly*, or even a (5A-6B+1G) *butterfly* and still have a *balanced butterfly combination*, but the further the *stretch*, the greater the *skew*. Notice that one side of the *butterfly combinations* created will remain *skinny* with the middle options positioned nearest the *at-the-money strike* price. These combinations will incorporate a greater number of *vertical debit spreads,* as the long upper-*strike* becomes farther removed from the interior *short-option strike* to balance the *butterfly* profile."

"It should be noted that the *skew* can be positioned on either side of the middle *short* options. So with C positioned nearest the *at-the-money* underlying *strike* price, one can create a (1A-3C +2D) *balanced-skewed skinny-butterfly combination*, or one can create a (2B-3C+1E) *balanced-skewed skinny-butterfly combination.* Effectively the results are similar using either *combination*, and the risks are similar."

"I have successfully traded (20-21+1), (100-101+1), and even (200-201+1) ratio *balanced-skewed skinny-butterfly combinations*, and received a *credit* upon entering these *long butterfly* positions. The resulting fills have been jaw-dropping to say the least. It appears that the larger the number of *option* contracts incorporated into the *butterfly,* the greater the *credit* received both upon trade entry and upon trade exit. These large *credits* do not occur for every trade request, but do happen often enough to really move the needle on increasing one's account value. Sometimes one has to be patient and wait a bit to receive order fills. More often than not the result is worth the wait."

"It should be noted that there is a limit to how far one might stretch the *skew*. As a general rule, the farther removed the extended *option* from the *at-the-money strike-price*, either in-*the-money* or *out-of-the-money,* the less actively traded it becomes. So there is a "sweet spot" for obtaining the greatest gains and/or number of fills. This "sweet spot" varies from underlying asset to underlying asset, and in general the higher the trading price of the underlying asset, the greater the acceptable *skew*. So with NDX trading at $12,000 per share, the (200-201+1) ratio *butterfly* becomes possible, while with SPX trading at $3,000 per share, a (20-21+1) ratio *butterfly* is better suited."

"The Think-or-Swim Trade-Ticket Interface permits a maximum of 99,998 *spreads* or *combinations* per order. For *balanced skinny-butterfly combinations,* that looks like (99,998A-199,996B

+99,998C) symbolically.

"If the *balanced combinations* are *skewed*, more contracts per order are permitted. Consider the (20-21+1) ratio *balanced-skewed skinny-butterfly combination* taken to the maximum limit. That would look like (1,999,960A-2,099,958B-99,998W) symbolically, incorporating 3,799,924 more *option* contracts per order than for the simple *balanced butterfly combinations.* Think-or-Swim, in fact, has accepted an order of this size and greater. So it might be said that *skewing* is a way to increase the *leverage* of trade orders. Employing *skewing* makes the journey to a trillion dollar account value a much quicker process."

"I usually place *limit-buy orders* for *balanced-skewed skinny-butterfly combinations* bidding $0.00 and commonly get filled for a *credit.* The *credit* can sometimes be sizable. Receiving a *credit* for buying into a position means there is no *negative* impact on my account *buying power.* Theoretically, there is no limit to the number of such buy orders that can be placed."

"I now wish to return to the topic of *bid-ask spreads* briefly." Dr. Nelson said. "As one studies the progression from *single option* trades, to *vertical spreads, to skinny-butterfly combinations, to balanced-skewed skinny-butterfly combinations,* an interesting pattern emerges. The *bid-ask spread* width increases. If positioned at or near the *at-the-money* price, the quoted *bid* price becomes increasingly *negative.*"

"For example," Dr. Nelson continued. "With NDX trading at the $12,000 price, the following price quotes were offered. All quotes are for *at-the-money call-option* trades for the closest expiration date. The single *call* option carried a $9.80 *bid* and a $11.85 *ask.* The *vertical spread* carried a $0.80 *bid* and a $4.75 *ask.* The *skinny-butterfly combination* carried a -$3.25 *bid* and a $4.75 *ask.* And the (35-36+1) ratio *balanced-skewed skinny-butterfly combination* carried a -$233.15 *bid* and a $337.05 *ask.*"

"Notice how the *bid-ask spread* width increases as the number of *option* contracts incorporated in the combination increases. A retail investor using *market orders* must overcome a $205 disadvantage before realizing a profit when trading one NDX *single-naked call* option. A retail investor using m*arket orders* must overcome a $57,020 disadvantage before realizing a profit when trading one NDX *balanced-skewed skinny-butterfly combination* incorporating 72 *call* options."

"In summation, the *Money-Catcher Strategy* is best used employing l*imit-buy and limit-sell orders.* The wider the b*id-ask spread,* the greater the disadvantage for retail traders using *market orders.* Use of *limit orders* can turn this disadvantage into a sizable advantage."

"As I suggested to you earlier," Dr. Nelson continued. "The *bid-ask spread* can be thought of as the *trade-negotiation zone.* The narrower the zone, the better the chances for obtaining order fills, but the smaller the profit potential. Conversely, the wider the zone, the lesser the chance for obtaining order fills, but the greater the profit potential."

"Not only is the *bid-ask spread* wider when *higher-order combinations* are traded," Dr. Nelson continued. "But the *bid price* becomes increasingly *negative.* This suggests that *long* or *debit combinations* might be purchased for a *credit,* if one is patient. I have had considerable success at employing *limit-orders* to buy *higher-order combinations* bidding $0 *debit.* These usually are filled for a *credit,* sometimes a substantial one. Conversely, I have closed these positions asking $0 *credit* and received sizable *credits* beyond my *ask.* This might sound too good to be believed, but consider the size of "wiggle room" between the quoted *bid* and *ask* prices. One can enter a trade position for a *credit,* a *debit,* or *at no coast,* and still have plenty of room to capture a profit."

CHAPTER 14

"The *long skinny-butterfly combination* and *long balanced-skewed skinny-butterfly combination,* when bidding for a *credit*, are examples of *Arbitrage* trades." Dr. Nelson said. "I am by no means an expert or authority in understanding how this works. I just accidentally stumbled upon a trading method that it turns out appears to employ
Arbitrage. Upon experiencing its success, I have continued to explore where such a trading approach might lead. So what is *Arbitrage*?"

"By definition, *Arbitrage* is the simultaneous buying and selling of securities in different markets, or in derivative forms, to take advantage of differing prices for the same asset." One session participant answered.

"Excellent answer!" Dr. Nelson encouraged. "As fancy as that sounds, it pretty much boils down to taking advantage of pricing inefficiencies which appear and disappear daily, and somewhat randomly, in actively traded markets. It may best describe what is going on behind the scenes with the types of trades I have been using. As an applied person basically, I am often lost as to what is the theoretical cause behind what works. I do not set out with the intention of chasing pricing inefficiencies. I simply request a small profit from non-directional *combination* trades. The rest takes care of itself"

"From a purely logical point of view," Dr. Nelson continued. "It does not appear possible to earn a profit from what I am practicing. Why would anyone offer to pay me more than $5.00 for a *spread* that is only worth $5.00? I do not have a clear answer for this. I do not know the mechanics behind how orders are filled. All I know is that prices are often quoted at values that ordinarily would seem impossible."

"When I make an order request slightly above or below the *spread* or *combination* value, more often than not my order gets filled. As stated earlier, this phenomenon only seems to work with *options* associated with a handful of stocks and market indexes. I have tried this approach on many other actively traded stocks and have had no success in getting my orders filled. Markets are emotion driven and are not logical. Evidently, perfect pricing does not exist."

"So, is *Arbitrage* trading legal?" Dr. Nelson asked rhetorically.

"According to *Investopedia.com*: *Arbitrage trading is not only legal in the United States, but is encouraged, as it contributes to market efficiency. Furthermore, arbitrageurs also serve a useful purpose by acting as intermediaries, providing liquidity in different markets.*"

"Regardless of whether or not one understands the details and intricacies behind the unconventional trading approach presented here, it always pays to go with what works. We can simply defer to a set of acceptable rules to make it operational. Indeed, one does not have to know how an internal combustion engine operates to succeed at operating a motor vehicle."

CHAPTER 15

"Today I will conclude our instructional journey." Dr. Nelson opened the session. "The *Money-Catcher Strategy* will now become yours to improve upon and automate. Before I conclude, I want to provide a few examples showcasing the *Money-Catcher* potential. This is intended to be fun! But prepare for some big numbers!"

"It took more than seven months to achieve the trillion dollar profit goal in a real trading account. I proceeded with caution, because I was dealing with unknown potential consequences. The extraordinarily large leverage of the trades required to get to that level of profit, meant the methodology had to be essentially mistake free. One slight mishap could blow out my trading account by putting me into a position that I could likely never recover from."

"That said," Dr. Nelson continued. "I have experimented with the *Money-Catcher* in simulation accounts, to test its limits and to observe what works and what doesn't. The following will highlight my experiences"

"We begin with *case study number one.*"

"The magic happened on the first three trading days of this trading year, and the bulk of the gains came from employing repeated *balanced-skewed skinny-butterfly combination* trades. The daily profit gains were as follows: on January 3rd, over \$304 billion; on January 4th, over \$90 billion; on January 5th, over \$695 billion. The numbers are rounded to the nearest billion dollars to simplify the presentation."

"Approximately 100 *round-trip trades* were successfully filled per trading day using the maximum allowed number of *combinations* per order. A new high-water mark was notched in terms of profitable gain. My overnight orders to buy NDX *balanced-skewed skinny-butterfly combinations* were filled for a *credit* of $11,538.10 per *combination* on January 5th. That is nearly four times greater *credit* than previously received on a trade order."

"Prepare for some more big numbers!"

"A single NDX *balanced-skewed skinny-butterfly combination* yielded $1,153,097.40. I closed this position for an additional $2,659.40 per contract."

"Now consider that 99,998 *combinations* per trade order are permitted. A fully maxed-out trade order yielded $115,307,433,805.20 *credit* on the *buy side* and $265,934,681.20 *credit* on the *sell side* of the trade!"

"Consider further that I placed five overnight trade buy orders."

"These numbers are almost beyond comprehension for just about anybody. They certainly ought to grab someone's attention. Imagine going to bed with a few thousand dollars in one's trading account and waking up a millionaire having only placed a trade order of a single *combination!*"

"Let that sink in for a minute."

Pause.

"On to *case study number two.*"

"Bordering on the absurd," Dr. Nelson continued. "I notched a trillion-dollar paper-trading profit in *one* day. On January 26th, I completed 160 total trades, or 80 *round-trip trades.* The majority, or approximately 80%, of these trades incorporated (120-121+1) ratio *call* NDX *balanced-skewed skinny-butterfly combinations.* A total of over 1.2 trillion dollars in profit was added to my paper-trading account in a single trading day!"

"How about *three-and-a-half trillion dollars* in one day?!" Dr. Nelson continued. "I give you *case study number three.*"

"Beyond ludicrous, on the very next trading day, January 27th, completing just 36 total trades, 15 of which were *round-trip trades*, I surpassed 3.5 trillion dollars in trading profit in a single day! Five of these *round-trip trades* incorporated (120-121+1) ratio *call* NDX *balanced-skewed skinny-butterfly combinations*. A credit of $70,866.10 per *combination* trade-entry fill was received, and 99,998 *combinations* per trade ticket were *bid*. The entry-transaction orders were entered before the market opened,and fills were completed by 9:33 am. In the Eastern Time Zone, active open-market trading begins a 9:30 am."

"I was out of pocket for most of the trading day, returning by mid-afternoon to submit position exit orders. What a pleasant surprise to open my trading account to find what had taken place!"

"A credit of $70,866.10 translates to $7,086,610 per *combination*, which becomes $708,646,826,780 per trade-entry order (minus commissions and fees). Five time this number equals over $3.5 trillion dollars in profit in one day!"

"Another Trillion Dollar Day," Dr. Nelson added, "Or *case study number four*."

"Reinforcing my earlier achievements, on January 28th, I completed 201 total trades. Approximately 150 of these, or 75 *round-trip trades*, incorporated (150-151+1) ratio *call* NDX *balanced-skewed skinny-butterfly combinations*, again using 99,998 *combinations* per trade ticket. Over 1.4 trillion dollars in profit was received by 11:30 am, after which I took the rest of the day off."

"The *Money Catcher Strategy* appears to work best when *option implied volatility* is high. This often occurs during periods of market uncertainty and/or during periods of high trading activity. On the trading days that produced the greatest profits, volatility was off the charts. Said another way, each of the *case studies* just mentioned had one factor in common...extremely high volatility."

CHAPTER 16

"Thank you Dr. Nelson for spearheading our training sessions." Director Bailey began, as the Patriot Project transitioned to the second phase, the development phase. "Dr. Nelson will remain with us through the developmental and implementation sessions as an on-site supporting consultant. I will be directing the developmental sessions from here on, and these will be more hands on. So let me just say job well done, Dr. Nelson. I'm quite sure there will be questions to be answered as we go forward."

"Each of you, as a Patriot Project associate, has been provided with a personal computer terminal pre-loaded with a Think-or-Swim Paper-trading account and with log-on instructions. Your task for the next week will be to familiarize yourself with the *Money-Catcher Strategy* using simulated online trading both during active market hours and non-active market periods. You may work individually, or in groups, whichever best suits you. At our next inclusive group session in one week, we will compare the results."

"The objective of this exercise is to produce the greatest profits while eliminating risk. You are asked to make note of any variations, cautions, and/or improvements to the methodology. Note also the steps required to replicate and automate the process, as this will be our next task."

"With that, I will let you get started. As a reminder, everything you involve yourself with associated with the Patriot Project, including both physical and intellectual property, is to remain inside the secure area."

"Welcome back to the Patriot Project development sessions." Director Bailey commenced following the one-week practice session. "We will begin with questions and answers. Did anyone experience any unusual or surprising outcomes, or insights while the using the *Money Catcher Strategy*?"

Patriot Project Associate Murphy raised his hand and was acknowledged.

"I was surprised to discover how many variations of the *Money Catcher* could be successfully employed." Murphy said. "The training session specifically focused on *butterfly combinations* with *skinny* and *balanced-skewed* variations. In my experimentation, I found *condor combinations* worked essentially as well as *butterfly combinations*, maybe better."

"Excellent observation!" Dr. Nelson interjected. " *Condor combinations* are close cousins to *butterfly-combinations*. *Condor combinations* have four legs instead of the three legs associated with the *butterfly combination*. To establish a *long condor*, one might purchase one A-*strike* option, sell one B-*strike* option, sell one C-*strike* option, and purchase one D-*strike* option. Symbolically, that would look like a (1A-1B-1C+1D) ratio *combination*. Note that like the *butterfly-combination*, the *condor combination* is composed of a *bullish-debit vertical spread* (1A-1B), and a *bearish-credit vertical spread* (-1C+1D). The *strike* prices for the options bought and sold however do differ."

"Like *butterfly combinations*, *condor combinations* can be *skinny*, *balanced*, and *skewed*." Dr. Nelson continued. "They can be positioned *in-the-money*, *out-of-the-money*, or *at-the-money*."

"The trading results generated using *condor combinations* likewise were very similar to those obtained using *butterfly combinations*. I decided to focus on *butterfly combinations*, because three-legged trades conceptually should be easier to comprehend and replicate than four-legged trades. Also, there should be fewer opportunities for input and output error."

"I might be mistaken about this." Dr. Nelson concluded. "*Condors* might be conceptually easier to grasp than butterflies for some individuals."

"Any other insights?" Director Bailey inquired motioning to the assembled group.

"Time of day." Project Associate Brown added. "My largest profits and fastest order fills seemed to come during the first half hour of the trading day. Then things tapered off."

"Another excellent observation!" Dr. Nelson responded. "My experiences were similar. Here is what I believe is going on."

"When the exchanges begin trading each working day," Dr. Nelson continued. "The activity is exaggerated in comparison to the rest of the trading session, unless some market moving news suddenly breaks. The market makers begin matching buy and sell orders which include orders submitted overnight and held in an order queue. Until these overnight orders are exhausted, there is greater than ordinary activity, and with it greater volatility. These factors improve the functionality of the *Money Catcher* trades and lead to larger and faster profits."

"Because of this greater favorability of getting *Money Catcher* trades filled during moments just after the market open, I like to have several overnight orders submitted and waiting in the order queue. These are the orders that usually produce the greatest profits, sometimes surprisingly large ones."

"I might mention while we're here that I have succeeded in getting *vertical debit spreads* filled for a *credit* during this active period of the trading day. That means if I am buying the 45-*strike call* option and selling the 50-*strike call* option for XYZ, then the 45-*strike call* is priced less than the 50-*strike call* at the moment of order execution. Normally the 45-*strike call* would carry a greater price than the 50-*strike call*. So here we have an example of *Arbitrage* price dislocation."

"If I understand you correctly," Project Associate Clarke added. "You are saying someone was willing to pay you a *credit* for owning a *vertical spread* that could result in $5 more *credit* upon option expiration. Is that right?"

"Correct!" Dr. Nelson answered. "However, in my experience, the best chance for obtaining such fills is during the first half hour of the trading day."

"Anyone else?" Director Bailey inquired.

"Do *call-option butterfly combinations* work any better or worse than *put-option butterfly combinations*?" Project Associate Harper asked.

"Another excellent question?" Dr. Nelson replied. "It's good to know you were paying attention."

"In theory, there shouldn't be an advantage to using *calls* over *puts*, or vice versa. Of course, in theory, the *skinny butterfly Money Catcher* shouldn't work. Real world trading appears to favor *call-option combinations.* Conceptually, calls are easier to understand, and probably used more often for that reason alone. It should be noted however, that when *call combination* orders are not being filled, *put-option combinations* many times do get filled."

"Very good then," Director Bailey said. "If there are no other issues, let us begin outlining a programming strategy. But first, lets see how much in profits our top three Patriot Project Associates produced in simulation trading in one week."

"Project Associate Thor was our winner, producing just over $350 billion. Project Associate Brown came in second earning $280 billion. And our third place winner was Project Associate Kirby with $225 billion in profits. Well done Associates!"

"The daily average per individual was approximately $100 billion using the maxed out *Money Catcher Strategy*. Obviously, this is a workable strategy for our purposes."

"See you in the next session."

CHAPTER 17

In just three more sessions, the Patriot Project had a detailed step-by-step program model for implementing an automated *Money Catcher*. It focused primarily on options for the European-Style NDX exchange traded fund, and began by searching for options closest to the nearest expiration date. Scanning these, it selected *call* options centering the *butterfly combinations* as close to the *at-the-money* underlying NDX price as could be found. For NDX, it searched for *strike-price spreads* of $5 for *skinny butterfly combinations* when available, defaulting to $10 *strike-price spreads* as needed. It next stretched the upper leg of the *butterfly* $1,000 above the middle-leg *strike-price* and added 200 opposing *vertical debit-spreads* to form a (200-201+1) ratio *balanced-skewed skinny-butterfly combination*. It next maxed out the order form specifying a limit-buy order for 99,998 combinations for a limit-buy price of $0. To complete the process it returned to the starting point and repeated the progression.

Each progression through the logic loop began with a fresh scan of market parameters, thereby allowing automatic adjustment to ever changing market conditions.

When alerted of order execution, the filled buy order was inverted to form a limit-sell order asking $0 *credit* and automatically submitted. All orders were submitted as *good-until-canceled* orders.

Redundancy was built in to assure operational success in periods of extreme aberration. The *Money Catcher* defaulted to incorporating farther-removed expiration-dated options when present-use options expired. Further, the *Money Catcher* defaulted to incorporating SPX *call* options using (20-21+1) ratio *balance-skewed skinny-butterfly combinations* after a defined period of inactivity, or unsuccessful order fills using NDX *combinations*.

The week following completion of the *Money Catcher automated program* was devoted to testing and debugging the system components. Still operating in simulation mode, the performance demonstrated marked improvement over the human order-entry accounts. *Money-Catcher automated-system profits* grew three times faster with no associated user fatigue from repetitive actions. Daily profits as high as $3 trillion were achieved.

Confidence in the program grew with each passing day. And when the week was finished, it came time to transition to the implementation phase of the Patriot Project and to real world execution.

CHAPTER 18

"Today we begin real-world *Money-Catcher* operation." Director Bailey announced. "Your hard work and diligent effort has given us a viable solution to the monetary crisis now plaguing our beloved United States of America. Today we begin our return to prosperity."

"Dr. Nelson, you may have the honor of pushing the start button."

"Thank you, Director Bailey." Dr. Nelson responded. "Here we go. Three. Two. One. Bingo!" And with that Dr. Nelson initiated operation of the *Money-Catcher automated system.* Everyone applauded, excitedly patting each other on the back.

"Our system is programmed to start slowly so as not to overload the market. It will increase activity incrementally each day for the next week, or so. Your job now will be to monitor the results, particularly as to how they are impacted by the component modules you engineered."

As the first week of *Money Catcher* implementation progressed, daily profits increased accordingly. Daily gains of $100 billion, then $200 billion, followed by $400 billion, and $800 billion were logged. On the fifth trading day, the one-trillion dollar mark was reached. To this point no adverse market effects were observed from *Money Catcher* operation.

Logging $1 trillion per day was considered a victory and meant that returning the Nation's balance sheet to zero was possible and was only a matter of weeks away. It was decided that operation of the *Money Catcher* would take place each trading day until $1 trillion in profit was reached, after which the system would enter a resting mode and reactivate the next trading day. The system would reactivate approximately one half hour before market open and submit a limited number of pre-market trade orders to capture the greatest profits the market would likely offer that day.

Approximately one month after the initiation of *Money Catcher*, the first Government Accounting Report was issued. It showed a balance sheet improvement of just over ten trillion dollars. Media financial analysts were scratching their heads as they struggled to report the news. What could have happened to explain the sudden jarring improvement?

"There must be some mistake." One correspondent reported. "No country in history has ever grown their economy at such a pace without negative consequences. I'm expecting next week's revision to be a doozy!"

President Cotton was quick to take credit, even if the improvement likely turned out to be temporary. He called an emergency meeting of the Joint Council for Economic Affairs to get answers.

"Can somebody please explain to me what has caused the rapid reduction in National debt?" President Cotton boldly asked. "I need more information. The Constitutional changes we have implemented will take years to produce such results."

"Clearly the Patriot Project is off to a remarkable start." Chairperson Wilkens reported.

"Patriot Project?" President Cotton asked. "Remind me. What is this Patriot Project?"

"When you created the Bureau of Deficit Reduction," Chairperson Wilkens responded. "You officially approved the creation and implementation of a classified program we now call the Patriot Project. This program has been kept from public knowledge so as not to compromise potentially sensitive operations. It has been kept from your attention until now to avoid political complications for your administration."

"The Patriot Project specifically is focused on returning the United States to prosperity by reducing the National debt." Wilkens continued. "Should the project fail, our country will be no worse off than when you took office. However, the political smudge of broadcasting such failure would likely negatively impact your Presidency."

"That does *not* appear to be the case so far. The project is yielding results beyond expectations to this point. I would advise you to refrain from revealing too much to the public until we have further verification."

"Thank you, Chairperson." President Cotton said. "Do we have a plan for how to proceed going forward? Anyone?"

"Sir, might I suggest that once we achieve zero deficit, we proceed onward to create a Strategic Financial Reserve, similar to our Strategic Petroleum Reserve?" Director Phillips inquired. "We could begin by building say a $10 trillion surplus fund. This would be a huge bargaining chip for dealing with our national adversaries. Think of the possibilities. We could offer to provide infrastructure improvement to countries like North Korea in exchange for verified cancellation of nuclear weapons development."

"Good thinking, Director." President Cotton responded. "You have brought up exciting possibilities. I will run that idea by our Defense Department in our next meeting."

"Can anyone inform me who is responsible for the sudden success of this Patriot Project?" President Cotton asked. "I would like to meet this individual and shake hands."

CHAPTER 19

Two months into Patriot Project operation the improvement to the balance sheet was reported at just over thirty trillion-dollars, leaving just twenty trillion-dollars improvement remaining to erase the National deficit The pace of recovery was astonishing. With new spending frozen the impact of this improvement was even more powerful, and with it optimism begin to grow.

The United States re-assumed its position as leader of the free world, this time with a focus on sensible prosperity. President Cotton's approval rating soared, and he was well on his way to becoming the most popular president the country had known.

....

As this was happening, the *automated Money Catcher* hit an unforeseen snag. Monitored results of daily trading began showing end-of-day losses. These losses were not large enough to erase the total profits for the day. Nor were they evident every trading day. However, they did occur often enough to cause some concern.

It turned out that trades left open as their constituent options expired when the markets closed were causing the issue. This was not a big concern, because on most trading days the *Money Catcher* met it's intended goal of earning one trillion-dollars of profit and entered a resting mode unexposed to market influences. On days when the goal was not reached, some trades placed were still active upon option expiration. These trades were exercised automatically when expiring *in-the-money.*

Dr. Ben Nelson was brought back for consultation to address the problem after spending a few weeks off duty in his native West Virginia.

"It seems I was wrong in assuming the *Money Catcher* to be entirely risk free." Dr. Nelson explained. "As much as I wished that to be the case, it appears that there is no such thing as a risk-free trade. There is always a possibility for option assignment at expiration, even when using European Style options exclusively. Since we have selected options situated close to the *at-the-money* strike price of the underlying asset, or NDX, the possibility of having component options for our *balance-skewed skinny-butterfly combination* expiring *at* or *in-the-money* is pretty likely. Even when settled for cash value, the option *combinations* open at expiration could result in a trading loss. How is this possible?"

Dr. Nelson's question was rhetorical.

"Recall the wideness of the *bid-ask spread* for *balanced-skewed skinny butterfly combinations* for NDX. One could enter a trade near market close and collect a credit of say $100 per *combination*. If the market closes before the closing order for this trade fills, the limit-sell order is canceled, and the open trade position is settled as a market order. Should the closing *bid-ask spread* finish with a -$233.15 *bid* and a +$337.05 *ask,* as was demonstrated in a previous example, the *combination* trade will be sold for -$233.15 *credit* per *combination*, which is the best available *bid* price offered at market close. So the difference between a $100 *credit* at purchase and a -$233.15 *credit* upon sale is -$133.15 credit per *combination*, which is a *loss*."

"We can reduce our exposure to experiencing this kind of loss in a couple of ways." Dr. Nelson continued. "First, we can stop trading in advance of market closure. If the markets close at 4:00 pm eastern time, we can stop trade entry at say 3:30 pm. As a rule, this has worked well in simulation."

"A second way would be to situate trade combinations *out-of-the-money,* particularly during the later period of the trading day. Here, the expectation is that all option positions would expire *out-of-the-money.* Should that happen, the $100 credit per *combination* collected upon trade entry in our example would be ours to keep as profit."

"A third way would be to ignore the draw-down. Under present market conditions, profitable trades are exceeding losing trades by a significant margin. This may not always be the case, so it is important to be aware at least that the potential for loss exists. A corrective adjustment can be engineered at a later time without sacrificing current success. Personally, I believe this third option to be the best choice. We can and should ride our success for as long as it will bless us. It is the American Way!"

CHAPTER 20

"Today, I am happy to announce that we have reached our goal of returning the United States of America to prosperity!" President Cotton boldly stated in a nationally televised address to the American public. "Our balance sheet is now positive as of yesterday, and going forward our duty is to keep it so, barring any unforeseen national emergency. To that end, I am authorizing the establishment of a Strategic Financial Reserve, similar to our Strategic Petroleum Reserve, to insure and preserve our National prosperity."

"It is my honor to present to you an executive order abolishing the Bureau of Deficit Reduction and replacing it with a new Bureau of Prosperity to oversee the proper implementation of our new situation. I want to recognize and thank the Patriot Project for bringing about this positive change. The Patriot Project, by means I do not fully understand myself, is responsible for the retirement of our National deficit. Going forward, the Patriot Project will be relocated from the Bureau of Deficit Reduction to the Bureau of Prosperity. Because of their sacrifices and dedication, individuals involved with the Patriot Project will be recognized formally and honored at special White House ceremony next week."

"The Patriot Project will oversee the financing required to fund the
Strategic Financial Reserve. This administration is proud to have this fine organization of citizens on board."

It had been only 16 months since President Cotton began serving his term in office. No one had ever witnessed a government successfully retiring its deficit at such a rapid pace before. This remarkable turn of events boosted President Cotton's popularity all the more and ushered in a new era of economic expansion.

A whole new agenda of projects and initiatives suddenly

were made possible. Long overdue infrastructure upgrades were started addressing aging and crumbling highways, bridges, buildings, and airports. A new interstate high-speed rail system was developed and begun. Sustainable agricultural programs were expanded to support food production and address world hunger. Funding became available to address and support medical research toward improving health and well being. Energy initiatives were implemented to seek and promote safe nuclear options, and improve on renewable energy alternatives, and further the development of clean fossil fuel usage.

Just as suddenly a new world of possibilities opened up with expanding funding support for defense, education, robotics, artificial intelligence, space exploration, zero-gravity research and production, mining, oceanographic studies, environmental conservation practices, and alternative individual and public transportation methodologies.

.....

President Cotton held a special reception at the White House, as promised, to honor the Patriot Project Participants. Each member received an Honorary Medal recognizing his or her contribution to the overall effort. Dr. Ben Nelson was in attendance, and received the Presidential Medal of Freedom for spearheading the project initiation. He shook hands with President Cotton and engaged in light-hearted small talk, like the two were old friends. This was a private ceremony, at Dr. Nelson's request, and members of the Press were excluded.

Following the reception, Dr. Nelson returned to West Virginia to pursue other interests. He was allowed to keep a substantial portion of the trillion dollar earnings he acquired originally, the exact amount was undisclosed. Dr. Nelson put this money to use in support of worthy causes in un-publicized ways, as was his nature. Eventually, Dr. Nelson turned toward saving the American Chestnut tree as his primary focus.

The America Chestnut, formerly the climax species of the American deciduous forest east of the Mississippi River, was devastated by the chestnut blight during the first three decades of the twentieth century. Dr. Nelson took to planting hopeful mutations of the species on abandoned strip mines throughout the state of West Virginia, and extended his reclamation plantings to include the neighboring states of Pennsylvania, Ohio, Kentucky, Tennessee, Virginia and Maryland.

....

President Cotton was honored for his accomplishment repeatedly. New York City made President Cotton guest of honor in a ticker-tape parade. The cities of Chicago, Denver, Los Angeles, and Seattle also conducted parades showcasing President Cotton as Grand Marshall.
A Robert Cotton Memorial was proposed and approved to be located adjacent to the National Mall near the Washington Monument upon completion. Mount Rushmore soon would boast a new carved head, that of President Cotton. And President Cotton was nominated to receive a Nobel Peace Prize for stabilizing international economic affairs.

CHAPTER 21

It is said of mankind that its population can be divided into believers and doubters. Believers are like conduits that channel unexplained energy and creativity, gifts from a divine Superior Being, and transform these toward advancing the quality of life on this planet. Their vision is limitless. Doubters recognize limitations in all areas of life, whether real or imaginary, and view the human purpose as an issue of managing limited resources.

Dr. Ben Nelson exemplified what it was to be a qualified believer. He used his God-given talents to solve a problem. Doing so liberated millions of citizens of present and future generations from unbearable financial burden.

Dr. Nelson succeeded at accomplishing something that thousand of individuals acting before him were unable to accomplish. His light shined brighter than those of the doubters. Yet he felt compelled to remain a relative unknown. President Cotton's honors were rightfully Dr. Nelson's to claim. But they held little value to him. To Dr. Nelson, a life of independence held far more worth than the trappings of fame or fortune. And understanding how to acquire wealth was far more meaningful than actual ownership of excessive material possessions.

BOOKS BY THIS AUTHOR

A Man Who Saved America
2024
Basil E. Pinker

Paperback Edition
https://www.amazon.com/dp/B0CX1FKWRZ
Kindle – Premium Edition (Ad Free Content)
https://www.amazon.com/dp/B0CW1BT5YP
Kindle – El Cheapo Edition
(Moderately Seasoned With Shameless Ads)
https://www.amazon.com/dp/B0CWWVTDLS

During the first term of Robert Cotton's Presidency, with The United States of America over $50 trillion dollars in debt, and the rest of the civilized world in worse financial shape, an unlikely solution to an ever-growing budgetary imbalance emerged. Dr. Ben Nelson, an eccentric West-Virginia recluse, accumulated over one trillion dollars in stock-market trading profits in less than one tax year using a strategy he termed the Money Catcher.... and purposely failed to report these gains to the Internal Revenue Service (IRS). When confronted by visiting IRS Agents, Dr. Nelson, in lieu of penalty, offered to spearhead a collective known as The Patriot Project toward the objective of retiring the National Debt...conditionally. * Dr. Nelson insisted on the enactment of a minimum of 5 out of 7 proposed legislative constitutional changes before commencing his Patriot Project duties. But could the decades of corruption and malfeasance be reversed swiftly enough to save a dying democratic federal republic? * The Money Catcher, strategy held the answer. Could this strategy be enacted effectively and quickly enough to shrink and eventually eliminate the enormous National Debt? Was this even legally possible? Could this be achieved without disrupting the financial markets? * Within these pages the answers to these important questions as well as others are examined. Discover the powers of positive thinking, unity of purpose, and strength of selflessness. Embrace a vision for a future of brighter possibility as did A Man Who Saved America.

◆ ◆ ◆

MONEY CATCHER
How I Became A Think-or-Swim Paper-Trading
TRILLIONAIRE - *And Got My Account* DEACTIVATED!
2024
Basil E. Pinker

Paperback Edition
https://www.amazon.com/dp/B0CYTL5ZC6
Kindle – Premium Edition (Ad Free Content)
https://www.amazon.com/dp/B0CW1NGBVM
Kindle – El Cheapo Edition
(Moderately Seasoned With Shameless Ads)
https://www.amazon.com/dp/B0CYXNK17M

This book documents how I made the journey from a minimal starting-account value to over one trillion dollars in profits in my Think-or-Swim Paper-Money trading account, basically using just a cell phone to place orders. Along the way, I discovered how to improve on my original method, which increased profits and also shortened the process. What originally took nearly three years to accomplish most recently was accomplished in three days or less. * The Money-Catcher Strategy focuses on using Skinny-Butterfly and/or Skinny-Condor Combination option trades employing SPX and NDX (with European Style options) as the underlying assets. It was discovered that for high-priced actively-traded stocks and ETFs, higher-order option spreads and combinations could be traded for a credit both upon trade entry and upon trade exit. * Limit orders were used requesting a small credit to buy and a small credit to sell. These orders usually filled for better than the amounts requested. With no negative impact to the trading account buying power, virtually unlimited trade orders could be placed. Whenever possible, no open positions were held overnight. * Experimenting with various option combination strategies led to the discovery of Box Spreads with "locked-in" value. It became possible to capture this "locked-in" value using overnight GTC limit-sell orders. Arbitrage probably best explains the process leading to my trading success. * Eventually, I stumbled upon Balanced-Skewed Skinny-Butterfly and Balanced-Skewed Skinny-Condor Combination trades, which elevated trading profits exponentially. A simple buy order for $0 often filled for significant credit (averaging $100 or more). Sell orders for $0 usually filled for $100 credit or more.

◆ ◆ ◆

Gumpert's Revenge
2017
Basil E. Pinker

Paperback Edition
https://www.amazon.com/dp/1549950398
Kindle – Premium Edition (Ad Free Content)
https://www.amazon.com/dp/B0CX59F9KY
Kindle – El Cheapo Edition
(Moderately Seasoned With Shameless Ads)
https://www.amazon.com/dp/B076DV5RGW

EUROPE DISCOVERED!! Team America Makes History! This is how headlines should have read in the year 1970, when the

Continent of Europe was discovered officially...not by some self-important explorer by the name of Sir Jonathan Q. Europe...but by an unlikely crew of eight (Team America) brought together by a series of extraordinary circumstances. From the pages of the authentic expedition diary kept by one Team America member, Europe's discovery is revealed through the eyes of a sixteen-year-old Eagle Scout and his brave companions. From the innocence and integrity of Scouting, to the temptations and challenges of turning adult...an awakening takes place among our select group of explorers to mysteries that often accompany life beyond parental oversight, simultaneous with glimpses into unexpected fascinations of European culture and geography. What's unique is not so much the actual discovering, but how it came about and eventually was realized. Could all eight Team America members stuff themselves aboard a 1966 cream-colored Volkswagen Camper van for six weeks, while making their way through eight, individually-different, European countries...and survive? Interesting adventures, both physical and psychological, were bound to result. And much like life itself, with an ordinarily joyous beginning and often sad ending, the discovery unfolds with just enough uncertainty to keep everyone on their toes. Accidentally funny, yet unpretentiously heartwarming, Gumpert's Revenge is a treasure of irony and surprise...aching to be revealed.

Diary of an Instant Millionaire

2017

Basil E. Pinker

Paperback Edition

https://www.amazon.com/dp/1973297515

Kindle Edition

https://www.amazon.com/dp/B077H96PZQ

This book reveals a stock-option trading strategy which has successfully generated billions of dollars in profits in a virtual brokerage trading account, and as much as one million dollars in a single round-trip day trade. Also presented is a no-loss stock-dividend collecting strategy for generating 2-3% per week income. No matter where one's position on life's financial spectrum, useful information can be found on these pages.

Beyond Ordinary Income Investing
Earn 2-3% Weekly with Intelligent Dividend Harvesting
2017
Basil E. Pinker

Paperback Edition
https://www.amazon.com/dp/1973350955
Kindle Edition
https://www.amazon.com/dp/B077NY5D6C

Intelligent dividend harvesting is a method for collecting stock dividends more frequently than they are paid using conventional buy-and-hold investing, while eliminating losses in the process. Once losses are eliminated, even small gains, and especially ones collected more frequently, begin to pile up at an astonishing rate. Hence one can grow wealth, or grow toward wealth, faster and more confidently than using conventional investing approaches.

The Land of Bunk
2018
Basil E. Pinker

Paperback Edition
https://www.amazon.com/dp/1976828244
Kindle Edition

https://www.amazon.com/dp/B078VHV7ZR

The Land of Bunk is an epic poem fantasy with appeal for all ages. Bunk is more than simply a place. It is an obsession, an art form, a pastime, an industry, a kingdom, a religion, a delicacy, a philosophy, a way of life, a profession, a sport, an addiction, a choice, a science, a measure of wealth, and foremost, a dream with a shiny green motif. Adventure, amusement and enlightenment await those daring enough to cross its border. Enjoy the visit!

◆ ◆ ◆

BEST SELLING AMAZON KDP KEYWORDS And MORE!
To Help Aspiring Self-Published Authors Succeed!

2024
Basil E. Pinker

Premium Paperback Edition (Ad Free Content)
https://www.amazon.com/dp/B0D1NBD7DL
El Cheapo Paperback Edition
(Moderately Seasoned With Shameless Ads)
https://www.amazon.com/dp/B0D1N9C1SZ
Premium Kindle Edition (Ad Free Content)
https://www.amazon.com/dp/B0D1CV2FCZ
El Cheapo Kindle Edition
(Moderately Seasoned With Shameless Ads)
https://www.amazon.com/dp/B0CWFQNBVP

This book was created from a number of ChatGPT 3.5 queries. The purpose is to identify and share specific keywords and keyword phrases that are associated with successful book sales by authors using Amazon KDP (Kindle Direct Publishing). In short, presented herein are the keywords and keyword phrases that sell books!